W9-BAI-394

Dale Earnhardt

Additional Titles in the Sports Reports *Series*

SPORTS REPORTS

Dale Earnhardt

Star Race Car Driver

Paul Steenkamer

Enslow Publishers, Inc.

40 Industrial Road	PO Box 38
Box 398	Aldershot
Berkeley Heights, NJ 07922	Hants GU12 6BP
USA	UK

http://www.enslow.com

Copyright © 2000 by Paul Steenkamer

All rights reserved.

No part of this book may be reproduced by any means
without the written permission of the publisher.

Library of Congress Cataloging-in-Publication Data

Steenkamer, Paul.
    Dale Earnhardt, star race car driver / Paul Steenkamer.
       p. cm. — (Sports reports)
    Includes bibliographical references and index.
    Summary: A biography of the champion race driver who finally won
the Daytona 500 in 1998, after twenty tries.
    ISBN 0-7660-1335-9
    1. Earnhardt, Dale, 1951– Juvenile literature. 2. Automobile
racing drivers—United States Biography Juvenile literature.
[1. Earnhardt, Dale, 1951– . 2. Automobile racing drivers.]
I. Title. II. Title: Dale Earnhardt. III. Series.
GV1032.E18S84   2000
796.72'092—dc21
[B]   99-41537
                                                 CIP

Printed in the United States of America.

10 9 8 7 6 5 4 3 2

To Our Readers:
All Internet addresses in this book were active and appropriate when we went to
press. Any comments can be sent by e-mail to Comments@enslow.com or to the
address on the back cover.

Photo Credits: Reuters/Joe Skipper/Archive Photos, pp. 21, 29; Reuters/
Karl Ronstrom/Archive Photos, pp. 10, 15, 92; Reuters/Kevin Kolczynski/
Archive Photos, p. 49; Reuters/Mark Wallheiser/Archive Photos, pp. 68, 75;
Reuters/Rick Fowler/Archive Photos, p. 85; Reuters/Terry Atwell/Archive
Photos, p. 37; Reuters/Winston Luzier/Archive Photos, pp. 42, 52, 59, 78.

Cover Photo: Reuters/Joe Skipper/Archive Photos

Contents

Chapter 1

The Greatest Win

With eleven laps to go in the 1997 Daytona 500, Dale Earnhardt was in second place. He was hoping to win his first Daytona 500 after eighteen tries. Earnhardt raced hard through turn two trying to catch the race leader, Bill Elliott, when Jeff Gordon came up from behind. Gordon attempted to pass Earnhardt on the inside. As Gordon passed, Earnhardt lost control of his black number three Chevrolet. He bumped the wall and then bumped into Gordon's car. Earnhardt had to slow down to regain control of his car. Unfortunately, the speeding cars of Ernie Irvan and Dale Jarrett were coming up fast from behind. Jarrett ran into the back of Earnhardt's car. Earnhardt spun and was hit in the side by Irvan. After being hit by Irvan, Earnhardt's car rolled onto its side and slid down the racetrack. For the nineteenth year in a row, stock car racing superstar Dale Earnhardt had failed to win NASCAR's biggest race.

This was not the first time Earnhardt had come close to winning the Daytona 500. In fact, he had been closer in other years. Earnhardt had finished second by a nose in the 1993, 1995, and 1996 Daytona 500 races. The amount of time he finished behind the winner for all three races combined was less than one second. In 1986, Earnhardt was in second place in this 200-lap event when he ran out of gas with seven and a half laps to go.

Earnhardt, however, suffered his greatest loss in the 1990 Daytona 500. In 1990, Earnhardt was leading the race through the last turn. He was heading for certain victory when he ran over a piece of metal on the track. The metal cut one of his tires and the tire went flat. Derrike Cope and three other drivers passed Earnhardt on the final straightaway. Earnhardt finished a disappointing fifth. He sat alone in his car for a long time after the race before stepping out to talk with the reporters who were waiting. When they asked him what happened, Earnhardt said, "There [is] nothing you can do about it either. I mean, you can't kick the car, cry and pout, lay down and squall and bawl. Just got to take it and move on. We just ran a little bit short of luck today, by about a quarter-lap or so."[1]

The day before the 1998 Daytona 500, Earnhardt was hoping for some luck. He found it in an unlikely place. While visiting kids for the Make-A-Wish Foundation, a little girl in a wheelchair gave him a penny for good luck. The Make-A-Wish Foundation grants the wishes of kids who are very sick. These children are not expected to live long or healthy lives. Earnhardt took the penny and glued it to the dashboard of his race car. "All race fans are special," said Earnhardt, "but a little girl who's in a wheelchair that life has not been good to, giving you a penny and wishing you luck, that's pretty special."[2]

Before the 1998 race began, Earnhardt was asked why he had never won NASCAR's biggest race. "This is my twentieth year," he replied. "And I'm tired of answering that question."[3] Earnhardt was also tired of losing the Daytona 500.

Earnhardt started the race fourth. When the green flag waved to start the race, Bobby Labonte took the lead. Earnhardt kept his number three Chevrolet near the front. He settled in for a long afternoon of racing. Earnhardt took the lead for the first time when he passed Sterling Marlin on lap 17. He kept the lead until lap 37, when Labonte passed him. Earnhardt, however, stayed close to Labonte.

Dale Earnhardt climbs into his car on the starting grid for the Daytona 500 in February 1998. Despite establishing himself as one of the best NASCAR drivers in history, he had never won NASCAR's biggest race in his first nineteen attempts. He was hoping his luck would finally change in 1998.

He retook the lead eight laps later. Earnhardt finally gave up the lead when he went into the pits on lap 58. The race was moving along swiftly. The first quarter had been completed without a single caution flag.

Earnhardt continued to race with the lead pack for the next sixty-five laps. He regained the lead by passing Jeff Gordon on lap 123. This lead, however, did not last long. On lap 125, Ward Burton ran over a piece of debris and shredded a tire. This brought out the first caution flag of the day. With the caution flag out, Earnhardt and the other cars in the lead pack drove into the pit. Rusty Wallace left the pit first and took over the lead. Wallace's time in front, however, was short. After the caution ended, Earnhardt quickly passed Wallace. Earnhardt held the lead for seven laps only to see his teammate, Mike Skinner, take the lead on lap 139. Earnhardt would not let Skinner lead the race for very long though. In turn four on the next lap, Earnhardt passed Skinner. With only sixty laps to go in the Daytona 500, Earnhardt was determined to stay in front until the end.

"I was working awfully hard to keep the car in front," Earnhardt said after the race. "Most of the guys were trying to get around the other guys, and when somebody would make a good run on me, I'd go up high and stay there and try to keep the lead. I did that until the end. I was just working the mirror and working the traffic."[4]

Earnhardt fought off hard charges by some of the best drivers on the Winston Cup circuit for the next thirty-three laps. Chasing Earnhardt were two Fords driven by Rusty Wallace and Jeremy Mayfield, Chevrolets driven by Jeff Gordon and Ken Schrader, and Pontiacs driven by Bobby Labonte and Ernie Irvan.

With the end of the race quickly approaching, the leaders were planning for their final pit stops. Then, on lap 173, the cars driven by Robert Pressley and John Andretti tangled and spun on the backstretch. This brought out the second caution flag of the race. It also provided the racers with the break they needed to take their cars into the pits. Earnhardt drove into the pit looking for some help from his crew. They responded by quickly adding fuel and changing the two right-side tires. Earnhardt zoomed back onto the track in first place. Now it was up to him to hold on to the lead. "The crew just did an awesome job," Earnhardt said. "I was working real hard to keep the race car in front. When they kept me in front, I was determined from then on to get there first."[5]

When the green flag flew again with twenty-two

FACT

The first Daytona 500 was held in 1949 on a makeshift course carved out on the beach. Red Byron won the race. The Daytona International Speedway opened in 1959. Lee Petty won the first Daytona 500 held there. Today, the Daytona 500 is run on the same speedway.

laps to go, Earnhardt was in first place. The drivers behind him were racing hard to catch him. Each took his chances behind Earnhardt. Each time, however, he was able to keep his GM Goodwrench Service Plus Chevrolet in front. As the final laps went by, it was natural to wonder if Earnhardt was thinking about what might happen to him this year in the Daytona 500. "I wasn't thinking about what could happen," Earnhardt said after the race. "I was thinking about what I was doing and what I had to do. I was working to keep the car up front."[6]

With less than two laps until the finish, Earnhardt continued to cling to the lead. Then, Andretti got tangled up in another mess. This time he collided with the cars driven by Jimmy Spencer and Lake Speed. The accident brought out the third and final caution flag of the race. The driver who crossed the finish line first after lap 199 would win the race under caution. "I saw it in my mirror," Earnhardt said later. "I knew when I saw the white and yellow [flags] displayed together that I was going to win if nothing happened to my car by the time I got back to the start-finish line."[7]

While Earnhardt raced for the finish line, Wallace, Mayfield, and Labonte did their best to catch him. But as Wallace and Mayfield battled each other for second, Earnhardt began to pull away.

When Earnhardt roared through the fourth turn, he saw the car of Rick Mast ahead. Mast was racing a lap behind the leaders. Earnhardt pulled alongside and raced next to Mast. He used the lapped car to block any attempt by the other drivers to take the lead. When Earnhardt finally drove away from Mast, the victory was his. He crossed the finish line first. Earnhardt completed the final lap under caution while the fans at the Daytona International Speedway stood and cheered.

The lucky penny had worked its magic. After twenty years, Dale Earnhardt had finally won the Daytona 500. Speaking of his good luck charm after the race, Earnhardt said, "I'd like to take that penny with me to the rest of the races, but it's glued there and Lisa France Kennedy [who heads Daytona USA] says I can't have it back."[8] He could not get his car or the penny because the car that wins the Daytona 500 is displayed in the Daytona USA museum for one year after the race.

After taking a victory lap, Earnhardt drove his car down pit road. It was a long drive, and the pit crews from all of the other race teams were lined up to congratulate him. Earnhardt eased his car down pit road and shook every hand.

When Earnhardt entered the press room after the race, he pulled a stuffed monkey from behind his

After finally winning the Daytona 500, Earnhardt gets kisses from his wife, Teresa (left), and his daughter, Taylor.

back. He threw it on the floor. "Hey guys, I got that monkey off my back," shouted Earnhardt. "Now you can quit asking me when I'm going to win the Daytona 500."[9]

In his career, Earnhardt had won just about everything that can be won with the exception of the biggest stock car race of them all. Talking about finally winning the Daytona 500, Earnhardt said, "It took 20 years, and this is the greatest win of them all."[10]

Chapter 2

NASCAR Racing Basics

Not sure what drafting is or what the white flag means? Like all sports, NASCAR racing has its own unique rules and vocabulary. This chapter contains information to help you better understand NASCAR racing and the phrases that appear in this book.

Draft and Drafting

Draft. Draft refers to the airflow around a car as it races around the track. Because of the incredible speeds at which stock cars race, they encounter strong wind resistance.

Drafting. A driver who is drafting drives up close to the bumper of the car in front. By doing this, the driver of the second car is pushing the car in front and also being sucked into the lead car's airflow, or draft. This action helps both cars go faster. In addition, because the car in front is pushing against the wind, the car following uses less gas to maintain the same speed as the car ahead of it. A driver pulling out of the draft gets a boost from the lead car. In short, a slingshot effect is created. This effect makes passing easier.

Flags

Green Flag. The green flag signals the drivers to start racing. It is waved at the start of the race and at all restarts.

Yellow Flag. During the race, NASCAR officials wave the yellow flag (also called the caution flag) to inform drivers of problems on the track, such as a wreck, debris or oil on the track, or a disabled car. When the yellow flag is out, known as a caution period, drivers must reduce their speed. They also cannot pass each other. Track position is determined by the position in which drivers cross the start/finish line at the end of the current lap.

Although drivers are not allowed to pass during a caution period, they can bunch up behind the car ahead of them. So, if the race leader was ahead of the second-place car by half a lap before the caution, when the caution is over, the second car will be right behind the leader.

To end a caution period, NASCAR officials wave the green flag. This lets drivers know they can resume racing.

Red Flag. The red flag signals drivers to stop racing. This flag is waved only when there is a serious accident on the track or in the event of rain.

Black Flag. The black flag signals that a driver has broken a rule, such as speeding on pit road. When a driver is black flagged, NASCAR officials notify the team's crew chief of the penalty by radio. The driver is penalized for a certain amount of time (depending on the severity of the rule broken).

White Flag. The white flag indicates that there is only one lap remaining in the race.

Checkered Flag. When the race leader completes the final lap, NASCAR officials wave the checkered flag. The checkered flag signals the end of the race for all cars on the track, regardless of whether or not they have completed all laps. In this way, drivers may finish one, two, or more laps down (behind the winner).

Lapped

If the race leader is more than one lap ahead of a slower car, the slower car is lapped. A car that has been lapped once would have to pass the leader twice to take the lead.

FACT

NASCAR, the National Association of Stock Car Auto Racing, was formed in December 1947 in Daytona Beach, Florida, to combine the existing stock car racing leagues. Bill France was NASCAR's first president. Red Byron won the first season title in 1949. Today, NASCAR has twelve racing divisions. The Winston Cup Series is the premier division.

NASCAR Divisions

NASCAR has twelve racing divisions. They are the Winston Cup Series, Busch Grand National Series, Craftsman Truck Series, Winston Racing Series, Winston West Series, Featherlite Modified Tour, Busch North Series, Goody's Dash Series, Slim Jim All-Pro Series, REB-CO Northwest Tour, Featherlite Southwest Tour, and the Busch All-Star Tour. The Winston Cup is the top division. Drivers race in front of the largest crowds for the most prize money.

The Winston Cup season begins in February with the Daytona 500 in Daytona Beach, Florida. The season ends in November at the Atlanta Motor Speedway in Georgia. During the season, the drivers race nearly every week. Most racetracks host two Winston Cup races each year. For example, the Daytona International Speedway hosts the Daytona 500 in February and the Pepsi 400 in July.

In addition to regular Winston Cup races, NASCAR also holds two all-star races each year—the Bud Shootout (previously the Busch Clash) and the Winston.

The Pit

Each driver has a pit stop along pit road. The pit is where the driver's crew is stationed. Drivers go into the pit when they need gas or new tires, when there

Earnhardt hoists the victory trophy after winning the Daytona 500 in his twentieth attempt.

is a problem with their car, or when the black flag is raised.

Qualifying

Before each race, NASCAR holds a qualifying event. One at a time, each driver completes one lap. The driver who posts the fastest time for that lap starts the race in first. The first starting position is called the pole position, or simply "the pole." The other drivers fill in the remaining starting positions in descending order, according to their qualifying time.

The Daytona 500 is the only race that determines starting positions differently. For the Daytona 500, the first two starting positions go to the drivers who post the fastest qualifying lap. The remaining starting positions are determined through two 125-mile qualifying races. The drivers are split into two groups, and the qualifying races are held on the Thursday before the race. Starting positions for the qualifying races are determined by a traditional qualifying lap.

Stock Cars

When NASCAR was created, its founders decided that the cars raced should resemble what Americans drove (stock cars). In this way, people could relate to the cars being raced. Stock car racing is the only major form of track racing that is restricted to

American-made automobiles. Although stock cars may look like cars driven on the open road, they are far from your typical car. Stock cars have a driver's seat only, no doors, a great deal of safety equipment, and very powerful engines. These cars can reach speeds of 200 miles (320 kilometers) per hour.

Tight and Loose

Tight and *loose* are terms that drivers use to describe how their car is handling. If a car is tight, the car's front end pushes toward the outside wall. This pushing requires the driver to oversteer to the left.

If a car is loose, it does not respond well when the driver turns the steering wheel. The rear of the car slides up toward the wall when the car speeds through turns.

Victory Lane

After the race, the winner drives into Victory Lane. Victory lane is usually in the infield of the racetrack. NASCAR presents the check and trophy to its winning driver here. The winning driver also poses for pictures in Victory Lane.

Chapter 3

The Dream

Ralph Dale Earnhardt was born on April 29, 1951, in the small mill town of Kannapolis, North Carolina. His family called him Dale. Dale's dad, Ralph Earnhardt, Sr., was a hero in his hometown. Ralph became a legend competing in the NASCAR Sportsman Series. He won hundreds of races on the small dirt tracks of North and South Carolina in the 1950s. In 1956, Ralph Earnhardt, Sr., won the NASCAR Late Model Sportsman Championship. Today, the Late Model Sportsman Series is known as the Busch Grand National Series.

Ralph Earnhardt, Sr., competed briefly in the Grand National Series, known today as the Winston Cup Series. He preferred, however, to race in the Sportsman Series. By racing in the Sportsman Series,

Ralph could be his own man. He was the owner, mechanic, and driver of his car. Ralph Earnhardt, Sr., was a full-time racer who worked on cars in the auto shop behind his house. Speaking of his dad, Dale said, "He worked in the shop all during the winter and all, on people's cars as a mechanic, but he was a full-time racer."[1]

Ralph and Martha Earnhardt had five children, Kathy, Kay, Ralph "Dale", Randy, and Dennis. As a boy, Dale and his two brothers played with toy cars on the floor of their dad's auto shop. Dale's bedroom was in the back of the house. He would fall asleep at night to the sounds of his dad working on cars. It did not take Dale long to know what he wanted to be when he grew up. "Being a race driver is all I ever wanted to be," he said.[2]

As Dale grew up, he spent more time in the auto shop watching and helping his dad. "I learned so much from just being around," Earnhardt recalled later. "I watched him build cars and engines, and I went to races with him. He'd use soapstone to draw suspension geometries on the floor and show me how things worked."[3]

Dale was so interested in racing that he dropped out of school in the ninth grade at only sixteen years old. "I couldn't sit in class and keep my mind on reading, writing, and arithmetic." said Earnhardt.

"Not when there were race cars at home to be worked on. I had cars on my mind."[4] Ralph Earnhardt was not happy about his son's decision. He had left school after eighth grade himself. Ralph knew how tough it was to make it in the world without a proper education. "It was the only thing I ever let my daddy down over," Dale Earnhardt said later. "He wanted me to finish; it was the only thing he ever pleaded with me to do. But I was so hardheaded. For about a year and a half after that, we didn't have a close relationship."[5] Earnhardt would later admit that dropping out of school was one of the biggest mistakes of his life. "I thought I didn't need an education and I've been fortunate to do well without it," he said. "But I wish I had stayed in school."[6]

A year after dropping out of school, at seventeen, Dale Earnhardt got married. In 1969, his first son, Kerry, was born. During this time, Dale Earnhardt worked odd jobs. He became a certified welder in order to support his family and his racing career. Unfortunately, the marriage did not last. Shortly after the divorce, however, Earnhardt got married again. He and his second wife had two children, a daughter named Kelly and a son named Ralph Dale, called Dale, Jr.

Dale, Jr., never met his grandfather. In September

FACT

North Carolina became the twelfth state to join the Union when it ratified the Constitution on November 21, 1789. North Carolina is located on the East Coast of the United States. It borders Virginia to the north, South Carolina and Georgia to the south, and Tennessee to the west. The capital of North Carolina is Raleigh. North Carolina's largest city is Charlotte.

FACT

Heart disease causes more deaths in the United States than any other disease. The most common type of heart disease is atherosclerosis. In this condition, fatty deposits called plaque build up inside the arteries of the heart. A heart attack happens if the plaque becomes large enough to completely block an artery, or if a piece breaks off and gets stuck farther along in the artery.

1973, one year before Dale, Jr., was born, Ralph Earnhardt died of a heart attack while working on a car in his auto shop. He was only forty-three. "There isn't a day I don't think about Dad," Earnhardt has said. "Oh, I don't ponder it all the time, but he is always there. My dad is my hero. Everything I am is because of who he was and what he taught me."[7]

Just twenty-two, Dale Earnhardt was on his own. Following the birth of Dale, Jr., Earnhardt decided that if he was going to make a living racing cars, he would have to be a full-time racer, like his dad. At the time, he was working in a wheel alignment shop. "I just finally decided the only way I was going to get where I wanted in racing was to do it full-time," said Earnhardt.[8]

Dale Earnhardt's decision was tough on his family. They struggled to make ends meet as Earnhardt pursued his dream. He was borrowing money to support his racing career. Yet, he had trouble feeding his family. "When I started driving, I put everything else in second place," Earnhardt recalled later. "It's paid off now. But there were tough times and I missed so much of my kids' growing up."[9]

In 1975, Dale Earnhardt switched from racing on dirt tracks to racing on asphalt. His goal was to make it big in NASCAR. His brothers, Randy and Dennis, helped him by working on the car. They also

As a child, Earnhardt dreamed of following in the footsteps of his father, Ralph, who also competed on the NASCAR circuit.

helped him at the race track. But it was Dale who had the dream of becoming a successful race car driver like his dad. "I think about my car the last thing before I fall asleep and the first thing when I wake up," Earnhardt said.[10]

Throughout the mid-1970s, Dale Earnhardt struggled to keep his dream of becoming a race car driver alive. He was waiting and hoping for a break. From 1975 to 1978, he raced in nine Winston Cup races for five different car owners. In his first Winston Cup race in 1975, he started in thirty-third. He finished twenty-second.

Unfortunately, the strain of Earnhardt's career troubles took its toll on his personal life again. In 1978, Earnhardt and his second wife divorced. With growing debt and a troubled personal life, Dale Earnhardt was forced to rethink his career plans. Just as he was thinking about doing something else, he got the break he needed. Car owner Rod Osterlund had seen Earnhardt race earlier in the year. He liked what he saw. So, he decided to give Dale Earnhardt a car to race in the Sportsman race at the Charlotte Motor Speedway in October 1978. "When I was told I'd have an Osterlund car, that was a big thrill for me," Earnhardt recalled. "I was going to get in a top-notch car."[11]

Racing against some of NASCAR's best drivers,

including Bobby Allison, Harry Gant, and Dave Marcis, Dale Earnhardt drove to a second-place finish. Osterlund was so impressed with Earnhardt's performance that he entered him in the Winston Cup race the following week in Atlanta. He ran well again, finishing fourth. The next week, Earnhardt finished eleventh racing for Osterlund in the season-ending race in California. Rod Osterlund had seen enough. After the 1978 season, he signed Dale Earnhardt to race the full Winston Cup schedule in 1979.

Said Earnhardt,

> Man, I couldn't believe it. I was going Winston Cup racing, and I didn't have to worry about paying for tires or engines or beating out dents in the fenders. . . . The dream I'd had ever since I was a boy was coming true. It was like my daddy had told me once. "If you work hard enough, your dream will come true."[12]

Chapter 4

Early Success

Dale Earnhardt's career as a full-time stock car racer began in 1979. He was going to be racing in the Winston Cup Series against some of the best stock car racers of all time, including Richard Petty, Cale Yarborough, Bobby Allison, David Pearson, and Darrell Waltrip. Earnhardt was teamed up with veteran crew chief Jake Elder. Together, they were ready to take on the big boys of NASCAR. "I could see from the start that Dale Earnhardt was going to win races," said Elder.

> He had learned a lot when he was driving those Sportsman cars on dirt. Sometimes when he is running asphalt, he will pull them [sic] tricks like he's running dirt. And Dale is good enough to get away with it. He is willing to take that extra chance that a driver needs to win a lot of races.[1]

Earnhardt drove the number two blue and yellow Chevrolet owned by Rod Osterlund. He began the year by finishing twenty-first in the Western 500. The following week he finished eighth in his first Daytona 500. Five races later, Earnhardt finished fourth in the Northwestern Bank 400. It was his first top-five finish of the season. One week later, Earnhardt edged out Bobby Allison for his first Winston Cup victory.

Earnhardt and Darrell Waltrip battled each other most of the afternoon in the Southeastern 500 at the Bristol International Raceway in Tennessee. During the final pit stop of the race, Earnhardt's crew got him back on the track in first. Earnhardt raced hard to the finish. Waltrip was unable to catch up and was passed by Bobby Allison, who finished second. Waltrip finished third. Earnhardt was excited after winning his first Winston Cup race. "I couldn't believe it," he said. "They gave me the checkered flag, and it was just the most exciting time I've ever felt in my life."[2]

Earnhardt continued to run strong through the middle part of the season. Although he did not win any more races, he had five more top-five finishes and seven more top-ten finishes. Earnhardt was having the time of his life when disaster struck. While racing in the Coca-Cola 500 at the Pocono

Raceway in Pennsylvania, Earnhardt blew a tire. This caused him to lose control of his car. His car slammed violently into the wall. He broke both collarbones and was unconscious for several hours. "I thought it was all over when I hit the wall," he said later.

> I had blown a tire and the car spun completely around and hit the outside wall flush on the driver's side. The impact was so intense my head actually banged against the wall and my helmet broke.[3]

Earnhardt's injuries forced him to miss the next four races of the season. Despite the accident, Earnhardt came roaring back on the Winston Cup circuit. He finished fourth in his first race after the wreck. He ended the year by finishing in the top five in three of the last four races. Even though he missed four races in 1979, Dale Earnhardt easily won the Winston Cup Rookie of the Year title. Looking back on his rookie season, Earnhardt had only one regret. "I just wish my dad could have been here to see me," he said. "I think he would have been proud of me."[4]

With a season's worth of experience under his belt, Earnhardt was excited about his chances in the 1980 season. He was looking to win more than the one race he had captured in 1979. "Everybody talks

FACT

The 1979 Winston Cup rookie class was one of the best ever. Along with Earnhardt, the class included two-time Winston Cup champion Terry Labonte, Geoff Bodine, and retired driver Harry Gant. Through the 1998 season, these drivers had a combined record of 127 wins.

about the 'sophomore jinx.' Well, I think you'll see a lot of improvement." Earnhardt said. "Jake [crew chief Jake Elder] and I communicate better. Last year we both got hot-headed a few times. Now, we both know what the other wants, and that's to win races."[5]

Earnhardt began the season by passing Darrell Waltrip to win the Busch Clash all-star race at Daytona. The next week he followed with a strong fourth-place finish in the Daytona 500. Earnhardt's 1980 season was off to a good start. By the time April rolled around, Earnhardt had already won two races. He was also leading the Winston Cup points race for the season. In the history of NASCAR, no driver had gone from winning the Rookie of the Year title to winning the championship the next year. Earnhardt, however, was not worrying about the Winston Cup title. He was only interested in winning races. "I don't care about getting far ahead in the points." Earnhardt said. "If I win the championship, I win it."[6]

Then, right in the middle of Earnhardt's hot season, crew chief Jake Elder left the team. Twenty-one-year-old crew member Doug Richert replaced Elder as Earnhardt's crew chief. No one knew what effect the change would have on Earnhardt's season. Richert knew everyone would be watching to see if

Earnhardt did not always drive a number three black Chevrolet. When he began as a full-time stock car racer in 1979, he drove a number two blue and yellow Chevrolet.

the team could keep their hot season going. "We had something to prove," Richert said later. "We were supposed to fall on our butts, go down the tubes. We didn't. There was a lot of adrenaline flowing. We knew we could do the job."[7]

With Richert leading his crew, Earnhardt kept rolling. As Earnhardt battled through the long Winston Cup season, the veteran drivers did their best to catch him. Richard Petty, who was beginning to close in on the points lead, wrecked at Pocono. The accident knocked Petty out of the championship race. With Petty out of the points race, the title came down to a duel between Earnhardt and Cale Yarborough.

Earnhardt extended his points lead by winning the Old Dominion 500 at the Martinsville Speedway in Tennessee. It was his fourth win of the season. Racing in the National 500 the following week, Earnhardt edged out Yarborough for his fifth and final win of the season. The National 500 was run at the Charlotte Motor Speedway in North Carolina. This track is special to Earnhardt because it is located near Kannapolis, Earnhardt's hometown. "This track is where I used to sit on the back of my daddy's pickup truck, parked in the infield, and dream about winning Winston Cup races and championships," he said.[8]

The National 500 was a very competitive race. There were thirty-seven lead changes over the first 200 laps of the 334-lap event. Earnhardt was battling some of the best drivers of the day, including Richard Petty, Cale Yarborough, Bobby Allison, Buddy Baker, Ricky Rudd, and Neil Bonnett.

Neil Bonnett and Bobby Allison were the first drivers to drop out of the race, when they wrecked on lap 185. Richard Petty's day ended when his engine broke down with 100 laps to go. After Petty's exit, Earnhardt found himself battling Yarborough and Baker. Earnhardt, in the number two blue and yellow Chevrolet, was clinging to the lead when the three cars pitted with fifty laps to go. Earnhardt and Baker stopped for gas and two new tires each. In a longer pit stop, Yarborough chose to get gas and four new tires. Thanks to his speedy pit crew, Earnhardt got back on the track first. After the pit stop, Earnhardt did the rest. Yarborough eventually passed Baker to take second, but he was unable to catch Earnhardt. Racing at his hometown track, Earnhardt took the checkered flag for the win. "This feels good to win here in front of the hometown crowd," he said. "I've dreamed and thought about it for a long time. It feels great."[9]

Even though Dale Earnhardt had won the last two races, Cale Yarborough was not ready to give

FACT

Through 1998, Cale Yarborough was the only driver to win three Winston Cup Championships in a row. Despite winning 83 races, Yarborough's titles in 1976, 1977, and 1978, were the only titles that he won in his thirty-one-year career. Perhaps this lack of titles is due, at least in part, to the fact that Yarborough used to split his time between racing stock cars and racing Indy cars.

up the fight for the Winston Cup title. Yarborough won the next two races of the season. In the process, he narrowed the amount of points separating himself and Earnhardt to twenty-nine. With one race left, Earnhardt needed to finish fifth and lead at least one lap to clinch the title. If he could do that, it would not matter what Yarborough did.

As qualifying began for the Los Angeles Times 500, Yarborough quickly posted the speed to beat. For the season, Yarborough won a NASCAR-record fourteen poles. When it was Earnhardt's turn to qualify, he mashed the gas and took off. Earnhardt pushed his car as hard as he could. He drove deeper into the corners than anyone else before letting off the gas. Earnhardt's daring paid off. He qualified for the second starting position. Unfortunately, the race did not go as well.

Early in the race, strong winds caused Earnhardt's car to have handling problems. As Yarborough raced with the leaders, Earnhardt began to fall back. Then, on lap 69, Earnhardt pitted too early during a caution. The mistake put him a lap down. For the next one hundred laps, Earnhardt fought unsuccessfully to make up the lost lap. But just as things were looking bad, he started to catch some breaks. On lap 145, Waltrip's engine died. This allowed Earnhardt to move into fifth place. Then, following another caution flag on lap 151, Earnhardt was able to get back on the lead lap. As the pack of cars eased through turn four on their way to the restart, Earnhardt drifted out of the pack. When the green flag waved, he hit the gas. Earnhardt zoomed by four cars. Then, he passed Yarborough to unlap himself. Shortly thereafter, another caution flag came out. This caution allowed Earnhardt to close the large gap between his car and the leaders. When the race restarted, Earnhardt was ready. He timed the restart perfectly again. Earnhardt hit the gas and passed Yarborough to take the lead. "I was ready, and they weren't," he said later.[10]

Yarborough quickly passed Earnhardt. The two then raced bumper to bumper until the final pit stop of the day. During Earnhardt's final pit stop, mistakes nearly cost him the title. To start, Earnhardt drove into his pit too fast. Unable to stop in time, he slid into the pit wall sending his crew running for cover. Then, while his crew was still working on the car, Earnhardt thought he had the signal to go. He drove off the jack. His right rear tire was only held on by one of four lug nuts. Earnhardt's crew held their breath while he drove the number two Wrangler Chevrolet around the track. Everyone was hoping that the tire would stay on. It did. But Earnhardt was forced to return to the pits. When he

Earnhardt ponders strategy the day before a race. Earnhardt began his career with a bang, winning the Winston Cup Rookie of the Year Award in 1979 and capturing the Winston Cup Championship in 1980.

finally returned to the race track, Earnhardt had dropped to fifth.

Earnhardt did not make any more mistakes. He finished fifth. Yarborough finished third. Earnhardt had done it. In only his second year on the Winston Cup circuit, Earnhardt had won the Winston Cup Championship. "At the time I won that first one in 1980, I realized what I had won, but I didn't realize who I had beaten—I'd beaten Junior [Junior Johnson, Yarborough's team owner] and Cale," recalled Earnhardt later in his career.[11]

By winning the championship, Dale Earnhardt became the first and only driver to become Winston Cup champion the year after being named Rookie of the Year. At the end of the 1980 season, Earnhardt was on top of the world. Unfortunately, it would not last long.

Chapter 5

The Intimidator

Halfway through the 1981 season, Dale Earnhardt's world began to come apart. Rod Osterlund, the team owner who had given him the break he needed, sold the race team. Earnhardt said,

> I just couldn't believe this was happening. I had the five-year contract with Osterlund. We had won the Championship and had a rich sponsor. It had not been a good first-half of the season for us, but there was no reason to think something like this was going to happen.[1]

After Rod Osterlund sold the team, Earnhardt's promising career took a turn for the worse. Earnhardt did not like the way the new owner ran things and left the team. Earnhardt ran the last eleven races of the 1981 season for an old racing buddy, Richard Childress. Childress, however, was just starting his racing operation. Both Earnhardt and Childress felt that it was not a good time to team up permanently.

From 1982 until 1983, Earnhardt drove a Ford for Bud Moore. In 1982, Earnhardt won just one race. He finished a disappointing twelfth in the Winston Cup standings. In 1983, Earnhardt won two races and finished eighth in the Winston Cup standings. Although his performance for Bud Moore was improving, Earnhardt wanted to drive for Richard Childress again. When Childress approached Earnhardt before the 1984 season, the time was right. Earnhardt made the switch to drive a Chevrolet for Childress. Earnhardt also switched numbers. The new team would use the number three. This number was special because it was the number that NASCAR pioneer and legend Junior Johnson had used. Earnhardt was still driving the blue and yellow Wrangler car. Wrangler, a clothing company that makes blue jeans, had sponsored Dale Earnhardt since 1981.

Earnhardt was where he belonged. "We only ran 11 races together in 1981, but from that brief association [we] always knew we'd get back together sometime," Earnhardt said. "The chemistry was just there."[2] Earnhardt won only two races for Childress in 1984. Yet, he finished fourth in the points standings. Earnhardt was ready to battle for the Winston Cup Championship again.

Since joining the Winston Cup Series in 1979, Earnhardt had been building a reputation as a tough driver. He was known as someone who would not hesitate to bump other cars on the track, or "trade paint" to pass. Trading paint refers to the fact that after a stock car hits another car, paint from one car shows up on the other. Earnhardt was nicknamed "Ironhead" by other drivers for his attitude and racing style. In 1985 and 1986, Earnhardt's actions on the track sealed his reputation. Those actions also earned him a new nickname, "The Intimidator."

Earnhardt's first win of the 1985 season came on the half-mile oval at the Richmond Fairgrounds Raceway in Virginia. He raced up near the front all afternoon. He was battling some of the best NASCAR drivers of the time, including Darrell Waltrip, Geoff Bodine, Tim Richmond, and Harry Gant. Earnhardt grabbed the lead for the first time on lap 289 of the 400-lap event. He had a half-lap lead when he went into the pits on lap 364 for new tires and fuel. All of the top leaders, except for Richmond, also pitted. When Earnhardt roared back on the racetrack, he was in second trailing Richmond.

Richmond was gambling that he could win without stopping for new tires and gas.

Richmond was still in the lead when Phil Parsons spun on lap 380. This brought out the final caution flag of the race. When the race restarted, Earnhardt was on Richmond's bumper. Instead of waiting for room to pass, Earnhardt made room. He drove down inside of Richmond's car and bumped him twice as he muscled his way into the lead. Before Richmond could settle down, Geoff Bodine took advantage too. He passed Richmond on the outside to take second place. Earnhardt, however, pulled away and won the race.

"I had to make something happen because he wasn't going to let me by," Earnhardt said. "I got good traction when the race began again. He wanted the low groove and I wanted the low groove, but I got there a little faster."[3]

Earnhardt and Richmond tangled again in 1985. This time they were racing in the Busch 500 at the Bristol International Raceway in Tennessee. Earnhardt was leading comfortably with sixty-six laps to go in the 500-lap event when the cautions began to fly. After the final caution ended, Earnhardt found himself battling Richmond for the lead with twenty laps left. Heading into turn three with seventeen laps to go, Earnhardt banged past Richmond

FACT

Junior Johnson was a star in the early days of NASCAR. Johnson raced from 1953 to 1966. He won 50 races. After retiring, Johnson became a team owner. His drivers won 139 races and 6 championships. The most famous drivers to race for Johnson were Cale Yarborough and Darrell Waltrip.

again. Richmond hung on but was unable to catch the speeding Earnhardt. Earnhardt went on to capture his third victory of the year. "Bristol has always been an aggressive race track. A lot of close side-by-side racing," Earnhardt said. "Tim and I went at it and I was lucky to get by him."[4]

Earnhardt won his fourth and final race of the 1985 season a month later at the Martinsville Speedway, in Tennessee. Two incidents in this race added to Earnhardt's growing reputation as a rough driver. On lap 442 of the 500-lap event, Earnhardt was in second chasing Tim Richmond again. Heading into turn four, Earnhardt bumped Richmond's car from the rear. When Earnhardt drove inside of Richmond following the bump,

Making his way down pit road to Victory Lane after a big win, Earnhardt receives congratulations from opposing pit crews.

Richmond turned into Earnhardt's car. Earnhardt was forced to drive down close to the wall separating the race track from pit road in order to avoid crashing. The two drivers continued to bump side-by-side until the first turn, when Bill Elliott spun in front of them.

The second controversial move came at the end of the race. Following the last caution, Earnhardt had the lead. There were only three laps to go. Darrell Waltrip was racing in second. When the green flag flew to restart the race, Waltrip raced hard to catch Earnhardt. Waltrip caught him on the backstretch. But as they raced into the third turn, Earnhardt turned his number three Chevrolet sharply to the left. He cut the third turn tight, driving into Waltrip's path. Waltrip was forced to take his foot off the gas to avoid colliding with Earnhardt. Earnhardt zoomed ahead. Waltrip was unable to catch him again.

Earnhardt finished eighth in the point standings in 1985. But, his four wins were the most he had won in a season since 1980. In 1986, Earnhardt's aggressive driving style finally caught the attention of NASCAR.

Racing in the Miller High Life 400 at the Richmond Fairgrounds Raceway in Virginia, Earnhardt had the lead with just two laps to go. Darrell Waltrip was racing in second. He was right on Earnhardt's bumper. Waltrip managed to slip by Earnhardt heading out of turn two. Racing down the backstretch, Waltrip had the front of his car ahead of Earnhardt's Chevrolet. Then, as the two drivers raced into turn three, Earnhardt cut the corner too close. He clipped the back of Waltrip's car, sending him spinning into the wall. Earnhardt also lost control and spun into the wall. The third- and fourth-place cars, driven by Joe Ruttman and Geoff Bodine, were also caught up in the wreck and damaged. The accident brought out the final caution of the day. Before Earnhardt or Waltrip could drive their damaged cars past the finish line, Kyle Petty zoomed by to take the lead and the victory. Because the race would end under caution, Waltrip and Earnhardt were able to drive their cars around the track one more time in order to finish the race. In his defense, Earnhardt said, "I was just trying to dive back under him and didn't make it. I was trying to dive under him and get back in front. I wasn't trying to wreck him."[5]

After reviewing the race, NASCAR fined Earnhardt ten thousand dollars. They also placed him on probation for six months. Earnhardt appealed the penalty. NASCAR later reduced the fine to three thousand dollars and dropped the probation. Despite the complaints about the way he raced, Earnhardt continued to drive all out in 1986.

Darrell Waltrip (left) confers with a tire specialist during a break in practice. Earnhardt earned a reputation for being an intimidating driver partially because of a move he made on Waltrip during a race in 1985. As Waltrip was trying to make a pass, Earnhardt turned his car sharply to the left, forcing Waltrip to slow down.

He won five races and captured his second Winston Cup Championship.

After winning the title, Earnhardt received a call from the driver who finished second. It was Darrell Waltrip. He congratulated Earnhardt on winning his second Winston Cup Championship. Despite the incident at the beginning of the season, the two remained friends.

After the season, Earnhardt was asked about the way he races. He was also asked if he tries to wreck other drivers on purpose. "If I wanted to wreck someone on purpose, I'd tell them what lap I was going to do it on and the spot on the wall where it would happen," Earnhardt replied. "I race hard and close, but I believe in clean competition. I'm not changing my style."[6]

Fellow driver Phil Parsons summed up Earnhardt well. "I think Dale has some guys intimidated to the point where if they see him coming, they get out of the way. He's an aggressive driver and an intense guy, but I think I can understand where he's coming from. He wants to win. And let's face it, he's a fantastic driver."[7]

FACT

Darrell Waltrip dominated the Winston Cup Series from 1977 to 1986. During that ten-year span, he won 67 races and 3 championships. Through the 1998 season, Waltrip was tied with Bobby Allison for third in all-time Winston Cup victories with 84.

Chapter 6

The Pass on the Grass

Dale Earnhardt finished the 1986 season on a roll. He won two of the last four races of the season and captured his second Winston Cup Championship. When the 1987 season began, Earnhardt picked up where he had left off. He won six of the first eight races of the season. It was the best Winston Cup start for any driver ever. Unfortunately, controversy continued to follow him.

Everyone racing in the Winston Cup Series was concerned and angry about the way Dale Earnhardt drove. Talking about Earnhardt, Geoff Bodine said,

> I guess the tactic now is if you can't pass you just knock the other guy out of the way. There is only one Dale Earnhardt out here and we don't need any more. I guess I'm going to have

to get tough and start knocking some guys around if that's how they want to play.[1]

Earnhardt was unfazed by the talk. "I really don't care what they say," he said. "I'm not going to change anything right now. I'll do what I've got to do to win."[2]

All the hard feelings and controversy swirling around the Winston Cup Series in early 1987 were like a volcano about to erupt. It was just a matter of where and when. The eruption occurred in the annual Winston all-star race in Charlotte, North Carolina.

Twenty drivers raced in the Winston. The last nineteen drivers to win a Winston Cup race and the driver who won the Winston Open earlier in the day participated in the race. The race did not count towards the season points total. The Winston was run in three segments. The first was seventy-five laps, the second was fifty laps, and the third was ten laps. After each segment, the drivers took a ten-minute break. The winner of each segment won money, with the winner of the final segment getting the most money. The starting order for the second and third segments was determined by the finishing order of the previous segment.

Bill Elliott, driving a Ford, had the pole position for the Winston. Tim Richmond was next to him in second. Behind them were Davey Allison starting third and Earnhardt starting fourth. When the green flag flew, Elliott took off. Elliott cruised to an easy victory in the first segment. He led all but four of the seventy-five laps. The only time Elliott lost the lead was when he stopped in the pits.

Elliott continued to blow away the competition in the next segment. He led all fifty laps on his way to the checkered flag. For winning the first two segments and leading the most laps, Elliott won one hundred thousand dollars. The driver who won the final segment of the Winston would collect two hundred thousand dollars. The final segment was a ten-lap sprint. Anything could happen during this part of the race. And it did.

When the last part of the race began, Elliott was battling Geoff Bodine. Racing side by side into the first turn, the two cars bumped together. Both drivers spun out. Racing inches behind them was Earnhardt. Although he did not make contact with either car, Elliott thought Earnhardt caused the accident. Elliott was mad and looking to get even. Earnhardt described the accident like this. "Bodine chopped down on Elliott and then Elliott turned into Bodine. I saw them hook up and figured they would spin up the track. I stayed low and it proved to be a good decision."[3]

Earnhardt took the lead following the trouble in

turn one. Elliott, however, was not finished. He got his car back in the right direction and took off after Earnhardt. Elliott caught Earnhardt two laps later. He drove up alongside of Earnhardt in turn two. The two banged together and traded paint as they drove down the backstretch. Earnhardt began to pull away. Then, racing through turn four, Elliott caught up again. This time, Elliott gave Earnhardt his best shot. He turned his Ford sharply into Earnhardt's Chevrolet. Earnhardt was forced down the track and into the infield. When a race car's tires hit the grass in the infield, they lose the traction needed to keep the car going straight. Even the most skilled driver will usually lose control and spin his car when this happens. Earnhardt kept his cool. He kept his foot on the gas and tore straight across the grass keeping the steering wheel steady. With turf flying into the air, Earnhardt shot back onto the raceway ahead of Elliott. This moment would come to be known as "the pass on the grass." Talking about the pass on the grass, Earnhardt's car's owner, Richard Childress, said, "When a man can bring a car out of the grass like that he deserves to win. I'm proud to be associated with Dale Earnhardt."[4]

Following the pass on the grass, Elliott continued to chase Earnhardt. Once again, he caught him racing down the backstretch. This time, however, it

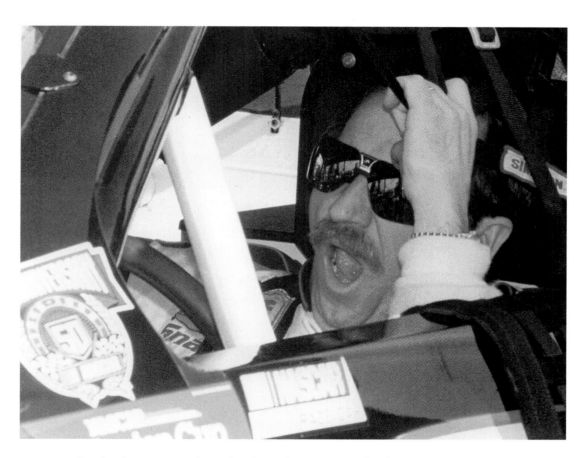

Earnhardt yawns on pit road as he waits to practice for the 1998 Daytona 500.

was Earnhardt's turn to play rough. As Elliott pulled up along the outside of his car, Earnhardt turned into him. Earnhardt bashed Elliott's fender as Elliott tried to avoid hitting the wall. Elliott was forced to let off the accelerator to avoid being driven into the wall. When he slowed down, Earnhardt zoomed ahead. Elliott tried to catch Earnhardt again. Unfortunately, his dented fender was rubbing one of his tires. Two laps later, while chasing Earnhardt, his tire blew out. Elliott finished the final segment a disappointing fourteenth. Earnhardt took the checkered flag and the two hundred thousand dollars.

After the race, Elliott was still angry. During Earnhardt's victory lap, he rammed his Ford into Earnhardt's car. After Elliott took his shot, an angry Bodine also bumped Earnhardt's car during the victory lap. Then, as Earnhardt drove his car down pit road on his way to Victory Lane, Elliot swerved at him again but missed.

After the race, Elliott was fuming over the way Earnhardt had driven the final ten-lap segment. He was convinced that Earnhardt had wrecked him on purpose.

NASCAR officials reviewed the final ten-lap segment of the Winston. After reviewing the race, NASCAR fined Earnhardt and Elliott twenty-five hundred dollars each. Bodine was fined one thousand dollars. Elliott later apologized for driving into Earnhardt after the finish. "I am sorry for what I did," he said. "It was unsportsmanlike, and I have apologized to all the guys on Earnhardt's crew. I promised that restitution would be made for damage on their car."[5]

Following the Winston, Earnhardt went back to work. He was looking to win his third Winston Cup Championship. Bodine, however, was still upset. Racing in a Busch Grand National race less than a week after the Winston, Bodine repeatedly rammed Earnhardt's car from behind. Earnhardt refused to comment on Bodine's driving. NASCAR fined Bodine fifteen thousand dollars for his actions. It was the largest fine NASCAR had ever given a driver.

Despite the early season controversy and the wild Winston all-star race, 1987 was Dale Earnhardt's best year on the Winston Cup circuit. He won eleven races and captured his third Winston Cup title. Fortunately, Earnhardt would never again be the center of controversy as he was in 1987.

FACT

Bill Elliott had won 40 Winston Cup races by 1998. He won the Winston Cup Championship in 1988. He has also won the Daytona 500 twice. In addition, Bill Elliott holds the record for the fastest qualifying speed. He set the record in 1987 with an average speed of 212.809 miles per hour at the Talladega Superspeedway in Alabama.

Chapter 7

A Seventh Championship

The 1987 Winston Cup Championship was the last title Dale Earnhardt won in the 1980s. It was also the last season he raced for Wrangler jeans. In 1988, GM Goodwrench became the main sponsor of Earnhardt's car. This was the first year that he drove his trademark black Chevrolet.

As the 1990s began, Earnhardt was ready to reclaim his role as the top driver in the Winston Cup Series. He won his fourth and fifth Winston Cup Championships in 1990 and 1991. After a disappointing twelfth-place finish in 1992, Earnhardt rebounded by winning the 1993 Winston Cup Championship. It was his sixth title. In the history of NASCAR, only one driver had won more Winston Cup titles.

Richard Petty, the king of stock car racing, won

an incredible seven Winston Cup Championships in his career. He is considered by many to be the greatest stock car driver of all time. Petty retired at the end of the 1992 season, after thirty-five years of NASCAR racing. For Earnhardt, tying the King would be quite an accomplishment. Talking about a seventh championship, Earnhardt said,

> You always want to win next year, and that's 1994. Going into the year and having the opportunity to race for that seventh championship is a thing that excites me. I never thought I'd be in that position, never thought anybody would win half as many championships as Richard Petty. Three was great, four and five, and now six. It's unbelievable to some point. It's exciting to look at this opportunity—and that's what it is, an opportunity. You can talk and talk about it, but you've got to get out there and do it.[1]

The 1994 season began like many before. Earnhardt came up short in the Daytona 500. He finished seventh. His disappointment did not last long, however. For the year, Earnhardt was never lower than sixth in the race for the Winston Cup Championship.

By mid-season, the battle for the Winston Cup Championship was between Dale Earnhardt, Ernie Irvan, and Rusty Wallace. Both Earnhardt and Irvan had won three races. Wallace had won five. But, because of some bad races, Wallace was in third place in the Winston Cup standings. Earnhardt was in front. Irvan, however, was only twenty-seven points behind. Then, on August 20, everything changed. While practicing at the Michigan International Speedway, one of Irvan's tires blew out, sending his car head on into the wall. Rescue workers found Irvan slumped over the wheel of his race car. Despite suffering massive injuries, Irvan survived the wreck. He would even race again. But, the accident ended the 1994 season for Irvan.

With Irvan sidelined, the race for the Winston Cup Championship was between Earnhardt and Wallace. Wallace kept the pressure on by winning three more races. This gave him a total of eight for the year. Still, the combination of consistent racing by Earnhardt and more bad races for Wallace kept Earnhardt in the lead. Heading into the AC Delco 500 at the North Carolina Motor Speedway in October, Earnhardt could clinch his record-tying seventh championship with a win. "We haven't got locks on the championship, but it looks pretty good," Earnhardt said before the race. "We'd have to do something awful dumb or have awful bad luck to lose it."[2]

Earnhardt started the race twentieth. Once the

FACT

Richard Petty holds the following NASCAR Winston Cup records: wins (200), wins in a single season (27), consecutive races won (10), top-five finishes (555), top-ten finishes (712), poles (126), laps led (52,194), races led (599), career starts (1,184), and consecutive years racing (35).

race was underway, he began moving his car up to the front. By lap 173 of the 492-lap race, Earnhardt was in the lead. He was battling the Chevrolets driven by Hendrick Motorsports teammates Ken Schrader, Jeff Gordon, and Terry Labonte. Schrader captured the lead on the next lap. Earnhardt, however, was able to get back in front on lap 297. Although he was not able to hold on to the lead for very long, Earnhardt continued to race with the leaders for the next one hundred laps. On lap 416, Earnhardt took the lead for good.

With the laps winding down, it became a two-man race between Earnhardt and Rick Mast for the victory. Mast had a strong car. He pushed Earnhardt around the oval, driving right up near his bumper. Mast was looking for a way to get by Earnhardt. Then, Darrell Waltrip crashed with fourteen laps to go. Waltrip's wreck brought out the last caution flag.

When the race restarted, Mast did all he could to get by Earnhardt. "I caught Earnhardt and I really thought I might have had a shot at passing him, but you know his bumper gets mighty wide there at the end," said Mast.[3] With one lap to go, Mast was on Earnhardt's bumper. Driving out of the final turn, Mast cut down below Earnhardt. He hit the gas and held on. Mast pulled up alongside of

Earnhardt. If the race had been fifty feet longer, he might have won. "Rick was catching me and I knew he was going to be a factor," Earnhardt said. "I didn't know if I could have held him off. I eased up in that last corner so I wouldn't make a mistake, and Rick almost caught me and got by me."[4] Dale Earnhardt had done it. He had won his fourth race of the year. He had also clinched his record-tying seventh Winston Cup Championship. "It's great to be No. 1 all the way around on race day," said Earnhardt.[5]

After the race, Earnhardt talked about his seventh championship. "I never thought I'd see one championship, let alone seven. And I can't sum any of them up in one word. It's going to take a long time to sink in before you've really got a grasp on seven championships."[6]

When talk turned to comparisons between Dale Earnhardt and Richard Petty, Earnhardt was humble.

I just tried to put it out of my mind of tying Richard Petty's record. I knew what it would mean. It would mean a lot to me, and I'm really proud and honored to be in the same group with him as far as being tied with him.

He's still the King. He's done it all. He pioneered it and got us where we are today. I can't take that away from him. I don't care how much I win or what I do.[7]

Rusty Wallace prepares to put on his helmet before a race. Earnhardt beat Wallace in 1994 for his record-tying seventh Winston Cup Championship.

Other drivers were eager to talk about NASCAR's newest seven-time champion. "In my opinion, Dale is the best pure racer I've ever seen," said announcer and retired two-time Winston Cup champion Ned Jarrett. "He's the only driver I've ever watched who I feel was actually born a race car driver."[8] Current driver and 1990 Daytona 500 champion Derrike Cope said of Earnhardt,

> What sets him apart is his aggressiveness and the great feel he has for his race car. He can manipulate a race car like no one else can. . . . He knows where the nose of his race car is. He can rub you without hurting you. He can do so many things so effectively to put himself in a better position without hurting you. He makes things happen and he puts himself in position to be there at the end.[9]

Of all the compliments Earnhardt received after winning his seventh Winston Cup Championship, the one that meant the most came from the man he had tied. Speaking about Earnhardt, Richard Petty said. "He might have won 300 races if he came along when I did."[10] Petty holds the record for Winston Cup wins with 200. Most of his wins came during the 1960s and 1970s.

Like Richard Petty and Darrell Waltrip had before him, Dale Earnhardt dominated the Winston

FACT

NASCAR awards points to each driver in each Winston Cup race on a sliding scale. The winner gets 175 points. Each driver to follow receives a specific number of points less than the driver ahead of him. Each driver to lead the race receives five additional points. The driver who leads the most laps gets five more points. The driver with the most points at the end of the season wins the Winston Cup Championship.

Cup Series. From 1985 through 1994, he won fifty-two races and an incredible six Winston Cup Championships. By winning his record-tying seventh championship, Earnhardt cemented his place in NASCAR history. Forever more, he would be known as one of the greatest stock car racers of all time.

Chapter 8

A New Rival

At the beginning of the 1995 Winston Cup season, Dale Earnhardt was the driver to beat. He was dominating stock car racing in the 1990s. Earnhardt had won the Winston Cup Championship in four of the first five years of the decade. To win these titles, Earnhardt had fought off many talented drivers, including Darrell Waltrip, Bill Elliott, Rusty Wallace, Mark Martin, Ernie Irvan, Davey Allison, and Alan Kulwicki. NASCAR drivers and fans were left to wonder if anybody would ever be able to slow Dale Earnhardt down.

At the end of the 1992 season, twenty-one-year-old Jeff Gordon started his first Winston Cup race. He finished a distant thirty-first. The following year, Gordon ran the entire Winston Cup season. He failed to win a single race. Yet, he did well enough to win the Winston Cup Rookie of the Year title. Despite winning Rookie of the Year honors, nobody imagined that this young man would be the one to replace Earnhardt atop the Winston Cup Series.

In 1994, while Earnhardt was charging to his record-tying seventh Winston Cup Championship, Gordon began to attract attention. The biggest event of the 1994 Winston Cup season was the first ever stock car race at the Indianapolis Motor Speedway. It was called the Brickyard 400. No driver wanted to win this race more than Earnhardt. Talking about the first stock car race at the famous Indianapolis Motor Speedway, he said,

> You get butterflies in your stomach and chill bumps when you walk out on pit road and look up at the racetrack. I'm proud to be a part of it, proud to be one of the first guys to be in the Brickyard 400—and hopefully will be proud to be the first guy to win it.[1]

Earnhardt, however, was not the one who captured the checkered flag on this historic day. It was Gordon's turn to shine. Jeff Gordon, who grew up in nearby Pittsboro, Indiana, surprised everyone by winning the first Brickyard 400.

All of a sudden, there was talk of Gordon becoming NASCAR's next superstar. Talking about Gordon in early 1995, three-time Winston Cup champion Darrell Waltrip said, "Everybody better do all they can do before Gordon gets any better. I think the shows over myself."[2] Even Earnhardt, who liked to tease Jeff Gordon by calling him "Wonderboy," could see that Gordon was a driver to watch out for. "He's the best young talent that's ever been out there," Earnhardt said.[3]

The 1995 season turned into a battle of rookie against veteran: Forty-four-year-old hard-nosed veteran Dale Earnhardt against twenty-four-year-old fresh-faced newcomer Jeff Gordon. By the time Earnhardt won his first race of the year in 1995, Gordon had already won three. Earnhardt chased Gordon all year long. The high point of the season for Earnhardt was the second annual Brickyard 400 at the Indianapolis Motor Speedway. Heading into the race, Gordon was first in the Winston Cup standings, Sterling Marlin was second, and Earnhardt was third.

In just its second year, the Brickyard 400 continued to be a big deal. "I guess in a way this is just another race toward the championship," said Gordon. "But this is definitely a bigger event than just any old race. It means a lot because of where we're at."[4] Gordon went out and won the pole for the race. He also broke

FACT

The original surface of the Indianapolis Motor Speedway was made of crushed rock and tar. That surface broke up during the first races and was replaced with more than 3 million bricks before the first Indianapolis 500 in 1911. This is why the speedway is known as "the brickyard." The bricks were later paved over, but they still remain under the track.

the track record for stock cars set the year before by Rick Mast. Earnhardt qualified thirteenth.

When the green flag waved to start the race, Gordon took off. His car was running well. He took the lead and held it for the first thirty-two laps of the 160-lap race. As the race wore on, however, Gordon's car began to have handling problems. Unable to keep up his early pace, Gordon lost the lead. He struggled with handling problems all day. He would not be a factor in the outcome of the race.

After Gordon gave up the lead, Sterling Marlin took over. Marlin kept the lead until Bill Elliott passed him on lap 51. The race was moving along swiftly. The first half of the race went by without a single caution flag. Earnhardt was running well. He was waiting for an opportunity to make his move. Elliott held on to the lead until a faulty pit stop on lap 100 ruined his day. Elliott's crew had trouble removing a lug nut from one of his tires. By the time they fixed the problem, Elliott had lost precious seconds. When he returned to the track, he had fallen into fourth place. Elliott would not lead the race again.

Following Elliott's trouble, Earnhardt found himself battling Rusty Wallace for the lead. Earnhardt was in second chasing Wallace when he headed to his pit on lap 128. Wallace stopped in his pit a lap later. As Wallace was exiting pit road,

Dale Earnhardt (left) makes a point to fellow NASCAR drivers Ken Schrader (center) and Ernie Irvan (right). In 1995, Earnhardt formed a rivalry with twenty-four-year-old Jeff Gordon.

however, trouble caught up with him. Rich Bickle and Joe Nemechek were exiting pit road ahead of Wallace. As Bickle raced to get back to the track, Nemechek pulled out. Nemechek ran into the side of Bickle's car. The accident happened right in front of Wallace. Wallace was forced to slow down to avoid the trouble. The few seconds Wallace lost cost him a lot. When he finally made it back onto the racetrack, Earnhardt zoomed by him in his black Chevrolet. Earnhardt passed Wallace before he could get his car up to speed. Wallace said,

> Until then, I really thought I had it locked up. I was thinking, "Hey, this is my race." But when I went to leave pit road and they crashed in front of me, it was just a roadblock. I couldn't go anywhere. Dale got by me during that, and track position was everything.[5]

John Andretti had the lead after Earnhardt passed Wallace because Andretti had not pitted yet. When Andretti pitted a lap later, Earnhardt took over the lead. Once in the lead, Earnhardt was not about to let up. He was driving hard when Jeff Burton spun his Ford in turn two. Earnhardt was right behind Burton when the trouble happened. Fortunately, he was able to squeak by without getting caught in the mess. The incident brought out the only caution flag of the race. When the race restarted, Earnhardt held the lead with twenty-four laps to go. As hard as Wallace and the other drivers tried to catch Earnhardt, they could not do it. Earnhardt took the checkered flag to win the 1995 Brickyard 400 by four car lengths. Wallace finished second. Gordon, the defending Brickyard 400 champion, finished a distant sixth.

"It would be hard for me to rank my wins," Earnhardt said after the race. "I've had some very special wins at places like Charlotte, Daytona and Darlington. We just needed to win again, and that alone makes this one special."[6] Earnhardt also poked fun at Gordon's age after the win, declaring that he was the first *man* to win the Brickyard 400. Earnhardt was hoping that his victory in the Brickyard 400 would help him win his record eighth Winston Cup Championship. He had something to say to the people who thought Gordon had already replaced him as the top driver in the Winston Cup Series. "We're not dead yet," he said. "Nobody's going to beat us by talking about it. They're going to have to beat us on the race track."[7]

For the remainder of the 1995 season, Earnhardt raced hard to catch Gordon. But as hard as he tried, he could not do it. Gordon won two more races after the Brickyard 400 before Earnhardt reached Victory Lane again. Heading into the final race of the season

FACT

Jeff Gordon is rewriting the Winston Cup record book. He had earned 42 wins by the end of 1998. Gordon is already thirteenth on the all-time win list. He is also the youngest Daytona 500 champion as well as the youngest three-time Winston Cup champion in NASCAR history.

Earnhardt wanted to capture the Winston Cup Championship in 1995 to prove that Jeff Gordon had not replaced him as the top driver in the Winston Cup Series. Even though Earnhardt won the final race of the season, Gordon still captured his first Winston Cup Championship.

at the Atlanta Motor Speedway, Gordon had the championship all but wrapped up. All Gordon had to do to win it was not finish last. If Gordon *did* finish last, Earnhardt would have to lead the most laps and win the race.

Earnhardt did his best. He won the final race of the 1995 season. It was his fifth win of the year. Gordon finished thirty-second—not one of his best races. It was, however, good enough to clinch his first Winston Cup Championship. Earnhardt had been denied his record eighth title. "Just remember us next year," Earnhardt said. "I'm not going away."[8]

Before the NASCAR awards banquet in New York City in December, Earnhardt took another shot at Gordon's age. "I guess milk will be flowing in New York instead of champagne," he said.[9] Gordon did not get upset by Earnhardt's comments. Instead, he had fun with them. At the awards banquet, Gordon had the waiter deliver two glasses of milk to his table to start the evening. One glass was for him. The other was for his wife. Talking about Earnhardt, Gordon said, "I've never seen him do any different to anybody else. He's always playing with everybody, and I think that's just his personality."[10]

Early in Gordon's career, Earnhardt may have teased him more than he should have. If he did, it was because he could tell how good Jeff Gordon was going to be. "The kid is a real racer," Earnhardt said of Gordon. "If I wasn't where I am today, I wouldn't mind being where he is."[11]

By winning the 1995 Winston Cup Championship, Jeff Gordon put an end to Dale Earnhardt's dominance of the Winston Cup Series. Gordon went on to win two more Winston Cup Championships in 1997 and 1998. Earnhardt was still shooting for his record eighth championship.

Chapter 9

Trouble on the Track

Dale Earnhardt began the 1996 season looking to climb back to the top of the Winston Cup Series. He finished second in the Daytona 500 to start the season. It was the eighteenth year in a row in which he had failed to win the Daytona 500.

After Daytona, Earnhardt won two of the next three races. He was first in the Winston Cup standings. It looked as if Earnhardt was ready to reclaim his status as the top driver in the Winston Cup Series. As the season wore on, however, Earnhardt was unable to reach Victory Lane again. By the time the Winston Cup Series returned to the Talladega Superspeedway in Alabama for the DieHard 500, Earnhardt had gone thirteen races without a win.

Still, he was in second place in the race for the Winston Cup Championship.

Talladega is one of the longest and most dangerous racetracks on the Winston Cup circuit. It is also one of two tracks where race cars are fitted with restrictor plates to control how fast the cars can go. The other track that requires the use of a restrictor plate is the Daytona International Speedway. Restrictor-plate racing was introduced in 1987 after a number of serious accidents occurred due to the high speeds the cars reached at these tracks. The restrictor plate is inserted into the carburetor in the car's engine. It reduces the amount of fuel and air that can enter the engine, which reduces the amount of horsepower. Less horsepower slows the car. Most drivers do not like restrictor-plate racing because it equalizes the cars' performance. When no one car is much faster than any other, the drivers end up racing in big bunches. Racing at speeds around 180 miles per hour in a big group can be very dangerous. One slip or bump can wipe out a dozen cars in an instant. "I guess that's what we've come to expect here," said veteran driver Geoff Bodine. "I think it's the most awful, dirtiest, nastiest, most dangerous racing in the whole wide world."[1]

In the 1996 DieHard 500, Earnhardt got caught in one of these dangerous wrecks. Earnhardt started the race fourth. His car was strong. He was in first place on lap 117 of the 200-lap race. Then, in an instant, everything changed. Racing into the first turn in a tight pack, Ernie Irvan bumped Dale Jarrett. Jarrett lost control and clipped the rear of Earnhardt's car, sending Earnhardt into the wall. After slamming the wall, Earnhardt's car spun and flipped on its side. Once on its side, the car slid down the racetrack. With no place to go, three cars rammed into the roof of Earnhardt's car.

After the wreck, damaged cars were all over the track. All eyes, however, were on Earnhardt's crumpled black GM Goodwrench Chevrolet. The race was stopped. Rescue workers rushed to Earnhardt. They lifted him out of the car carefully. Earnhardt refused to be placed on a stretcher. He insisted on walking to the ambulance that was waiting to take him to the infield hospital. On the way to the ambulance, Earnhardt gave a shaky thumbs-up to the crowd. He did not want anyone to worry about him. Thanks to the safety features that NASCAR requires, Earnhardt survived the wreck with only a fractured sternum and a broken collarbone. This was the worst wreck of Earnhardt's career since his terrible accident at Pocono during his rookie season.

Talking about how he survived the crash, Earnhardt said, "I held on to the steering wheel

FACT

Stock cars have many safety features that help drivers to survive wrecks, including a safety harness to keep the driver strapped in; roll bars that absorb most of the energy of the crash and keep the driver's cockpit from collapsing; window and roof nets that keep the driver's head and arms inside the car; a collapsible steering wheel; and leg supports that keep the driver's legs and ankles from moving, reducing the risk of injury.

practically the whole time. I was bouncing around in the car, but I was still braced in there pretty good."[2]

The wreck at Talladega hurt Earnhardt's chances to win his record eighth championship. Earnhardt, however, did not miss any races. He was able to start the next few races before quickly handing his car over to a replacement driver. In this way, he could continue to collect points based on where the replacement driver finished. It did not matter. Earnhardt failed to win any races in 1996 after the wreck at Talladega. He ended up fourth in the battle for the Winston Cup Championship.

The 1997 season began with another wreck for Earnhardt. With eleven laps to go in the Daytona 500, Earnhardt was racing in second. Then, racing out of turn two, Jeff Gordon pulled his rainbow-striped Chevrolet up along the inside of Earnhardt's car. Gordon's move caused Earnhardt to briefly lose control. At Daytona, that is all it takes. "Gordon came up on me and the car pushed off the corner," Earnhardt said. "I got into the wall, checked up, somebody hit me from behind. Next thing I know, we're on the roof again."[3] When Earnhardt slowed to regain control of his car, he was hit from behind by Dale Jarrett. Jarrett's hit caused Earnhardt's car to turn sideways. His car was then hit by the Ford driven by Ernie Irvan. This hit sent Earnhardt's car

Like his father, Dale Earnhardt, Jr., also had some accidents. In this wreck, Dale Earnhardt, Jr.'s car becomes airborne as it flies above the #64 Chevrolet driven by Dick Trickle.

onto its side. The car slid and tumbled down the track before coming to rest back on its wheels.

Earnhardt was taken from his car on a stretcher. But, as he was getting into the ambulance that was to take him to the hospital, Earnhardt noticed his car resting right-side up. "I got in the ambulance and looked back over there and I said, 'Man, the wheels ain't knocked off that car yet.' I went back over there and looked at the wheels and I told the guy in the car (who was preparing to haul it away) to flip the switch, and it fired up. I said, 'Get out. I gotta go.'"[4]

Amazingly, Earnhardt drove his mangled car back to his pit. There, his pit crew taped up the loose parts. When they were done, Earnhardt drove his banged-up car back onto the track. Although he had no chance to win, Earnhardt wanted to get as many Winston Cup points as he could. He was still thinking about that eighth championship.

Unfortunately, by the time the Winston Cup Series arrived at the Darlington Raceway in South Carolina for the Mountain Dew Southern 500 at the end of August, Earnhardt was still looking for his first win of the year. It did not come at Darlington, either. Earnhardt started a distant thirty-sixth. When the race began, however, it was clear that something was wrong. Earnhardt's car banged into the wall heading into turn one on the first lap. Leaving turn two, Earnhardt's car slammed into the wall again. For the next two laps, a confused Earnhardt drove slowly around the track looking for pit road. When he finally found it, he was taken out of his car. Earnhardt was rushed to the hospital. He remained in the hospital while the doctors tried to figure out what had happened. "They didn't check me to see if I was pregnant," Earnhardt said after the doctors finished checking him out, "but they did everything else. And they didn't find anything."[5] The doctors could not tell what had happened to Earnhardt. They could not find anything wrong with him. Earnhardt was given the green light to keep racing. He was, however, still troubled by what had happened. Said Earnhardt,

> One thing that concerned me about my health was my dad died of a heart attack. When I'm concerned about my health and what I may or may not be able to do from here on, the major thing was life itself and spending it with people who are close to me.
>
> I definitely wanted to find out what was wrong and what was going on. The thought did cross my mind that I might not be able to drive again.[6]

FACT

General Motors Corporation (GM) is the world's largest maker of automobiles. GM sells about one third of all cars and trucks in the United States and about one sixth of all cars and trucks in the world. GM sells cars under the brand names of Buick, Cadillac, Chevrolet, Geo, GMC, Oldsmobile, Pontiac, and Saturn.

Earnhardt did drive again. He finished the remainder of the 1997 season on an upswing. He finished in the top five in four of the last seven races and ended the year in fifth place in the Winston Cup standings.

Although Earnhardt's performance on the track was improving, he was caught in the longest losing streak of his career. Fifty-nine races had been run since the last time Dale Earnhardt had celebrated in Victory Lane. He had failed to win a single race in 1997. It was Earnhardt's first winless year since 1981.

"It seems that things are not as great as they were before the Talladega crash," Earnhardt said towards the end of the 1997 season. "I don't understand why we haven't won races this year. We were so dominant in years past that it's tough not to [dominate]. We'll get it right. I guarantee you."[7]

Despite all of his troubles on the track, Earnhardt was determined to make it back to Victory Lane. When the 1998 Winston Cup season began, Earnhardt did just that. Racing in the first race of the year, the Daytona 500, Earnhardt ended his fifty-nine-race winless streak. In his twentieth try, he finally won the Daytona 500. Dale Earnhardt showed everyone that his career was not over.

Chapter 10

The Future

Dale Earnhardt is a stock car racing legend. He is considered one of the greatest stock car drivers of all time. As of 1999, Earnhardt was sixth for Winston Cup victories. He was tied for first for championships won. After more than twenty years of racing in the NASCAR Winston Cup Series, Earnhardt does not have anything left to prove on the track. Still, the desire to win more races and that eighth championship burns inside him. "I can't say enough about winning the Daytona 500, but it didn't satisfy my appetite for winning. I want to win more races, and I want to win that eighth championship."[1]

Earnhardt has also found happiness off the track. In 1982, he married Teresa Houston. They have a daughter named Taylor. Earnhardt also remains close with his three older children, Kerry, Kelly, and Dale, Jr., who live near him in North Carolina. Kerry and Dale, Jr., race in the Busch Grand National Series. Dale, Jr., won the 1998 Busch Grand National Championship. He drives the number three AC Delco Chevrolet for his father and team owner, Dale Earnhardt, Sr. Talking about his kids, Dale Earnhardt, Sr., says, "I dearly love all my kids. I am proud of all of them, and my entire family. Every single one has made me very proud."[2]

When he is not racing, Dale Earnhardt enjoys hunting and fishing. He also enjoys working on the large farm that he owns. Earnhardt often gets up at dawn to hop on his tractor and go to work in his fields. He has said,

> This farm is my pressure release. Sometimes I walk all over the place by myself, and other times I walk out into the woods and sit down with my back against a tree and listen to tree frogs, katydids and bluebirds, and I watch the other forms of wildlife. I get a kick out of seeing what is going on around me.[3]

In addition to his own racing career, Earnhardt now owns several NASCAR racing teams. He owns a Craftsman Truck team, a Busch Grand National team, and a Winston Cup team. Talking about Earnhardt's racing teams, Don Hawk, the president of Dale Earnhardt, Inc., says, "It's a long-range business plan that we thought about years ago. Dale has had building championship teams on his mind for a long time."[4]

Earnhardt's own racing career is a separate matter. The big question is how many more years he will race. His current contract with team owner Richard Childress ends after the 2000 Winston Cup season. At that time, Dale Earnhardt will be forty-nine years old. He is not saying, however, that he will retire when his contract is over. "Right now, my deal is, I still want to win races, want to win championships, still want to win that other championship. I don't ponder on quitting or retiring or whether I should or shouldn't."[5]

Dale Earnhardt showed that he had a lot of racing left in him in 1999, however. He started the season with a dramatic second-place finish in the Daytona 500 and went on to win three races. Controversy, however, continued to follow him.

While battling for his second win of the season at the Bristol Motor Speedway in Tennessee, Earnhardt bumped Terry Labonte's car on the last lap of the race. The bump caused Labonte's car to spin across the track. As Labonte spun, Earnhardt drove by for the win. The incident caused an uproar among other drivers, the media, and the fans. NASCAR officials,

FACT

The Petty family represents four generations of stock car racers. Lee Petty raced for sixteen years in the number 42 car. Lee's son, Richard, raced for thirty-five years in the number 43 car. Richard's son, Kyle, races today in the number 44 car. Kyle's son, Adam, races in the Busch Grand National Series in the number 45 car.

Earnhardt crossed the finish line in first place at the Daytona 500 in 1998.

however, declared that Earnhardt had done nothing wrong.

Dale Earnhardt finished the 1999 Winston Cup season seventh in the point standings. He remains determined to continue racing as he chases a record eighth championship.

In addition, Earnhardt's racing team continued to perform well in 1999. For the second straight year, Earnhardt's son Dale, Jr., won the Busch Grand National title. Dale, Jr., also competed in a few Winston Cup races. He raced the full Winston Cup schedule in 2000.

Tragedy struck the Earnhardt family and the world of auto racing when, in an accident on the last turn of the last lap of the Daytona 500 on February 18, 2001, Dale Earnhardt was killed.

Earnhardt was driving his No. 3 black Goodwrench Chevy in a tightly packed group of cars that was chasing the eventual race winner, teammate Michael Waltrip. The accident occurred after Earnhardt attempted to block Sterling Marlin from gaining ground on Waltrip and Dale, Jr., and Marlin's car tapped Earnhardt's. Earnhardt's car then slid and bounced into the car driven by Ken Schrader. Both cars suddenly changed course. Earnhardt slammed into the wall, while Scharder's car bounced off of Earnhardt's. Earnhardt had hit the wall virtually head-on doing 180 miles per hour.

Earnhardt's son, Dale, Jr., came in second in that race. It appeared that, by blocking Sterling Marlin's car, Earnhardt may have been trying to protect the victory for his son, Dale, Jr., and Michael Waltrip, who were teammates of Earnhardt's.

Dale Earnhardt was a racing legend, known for his tenacity and competitive nature. He will not soon be forgotten.

Chapter Notes

Chapter 1. The Greatest Win

1. Frank Vehorn, *The Intimidator* (Asheboro, N.C.: Down Home Press, 1991), p. 242.

2. Benny Phillips, "The 40th Daytona 500," *Stock Car Racing*, May 1998, p. 28.

3. Paul Daugherty, "Earnhardt is Sentimental Favorite at Daytona," *Gannett News Service*, February 14, 1998 <http://www.elibrary.com>, March 22, 2000.

4. Jim McLaurin, "Earnhardt Ends 20-Year 500 Drought," *The State* (Columbia, S.C.), February 16, 1998, p. C1.

5. Shav Glick, "Dale Earnhardt Finally Breaks Through and Wins a Thrilling Daytona 500," *Los Angeles Times*, February 16, 1998, sports, p. 1.

6. Ed Hinton, "The Hunt's Over," *Sports Illustrated*, February 23, 1998, p. 69.

7. Ibid.

8. Phillips, p. 28.

9. Glick, p. 1.

10. Phillips, p. 28.

Chapter 2. NASCAR Racing Basics

No notes.

Chapter 3. The Dream

1. Kim Chapin, *Fast as White Lightning: The Story of Stock Car Racing* (New York: Three Rivers Press, 1998), p. 258.

2. Frank Vehorn, *The Intimidator* (Asheboro, N.C.: Down Home Press, 1991), p. 1.

3. Sandra McKee, "Earnhardt Slows, Takes Look Back," *Baltimore Sun*, December 2, 1994, sports, p. 5C.

4. Rick Houston, "Dale Earnhardt: The Road to Fame Was a Tough, Rocky One for the Intimidator but He Never Lost His Focus," *Richard Petty's Official Guide to 50 Years of NASCAR* CSM Group, Street and Smith's Sports Group and Petty Marketing Company L.L.C., 1998), p. 90.

5. Sam Moses, "Dale Turns 'Em Pale—Dale Earnhardt This Year's NASCAR Champion, Isn't Shy About Banging Fenders," *Sports Illustrated*, September 7, 1987, p. 32.

6. McKee, p. 5C.

7. Ibid.

8. Vehorn, p. 3.

9. Gerald Martin, "Dale Earnhardt, Hell on Wheels," *TV Guide*, February 15, 1997, p. S10.

10. Chapin, p. 253.

11. Houston, p. 93.

12. Vehorn, p. 9.

Chapter 4. Early Success

1. Frank Vehorn, *The Intimidator* (Asheboro, N.C.: Down Home Press, 1991), p. 12.

2. Kim Chapin, *Fast as White Lightning: The Story of Stock Car Racing* (New York: Three Rivers Press 1998), p. 251.

3. Michael Knight, "Earnhardt Aching," *Philadelphia Daily News*, September 13, 1979, p. 65.

4. Vehorn, p. 14.

5. Michael Knight, "Earnhardt's Ready to Roll," *Philadelphia Daily News*, February 14, 1980, p. 64.

6. Vehorn, p. 22.

7. Michael Benson, *Race Car Legends: Dale Earnhardt* (Philadelphia: Chelsea House Publishers, 1996), p. 32.

8. Vehorn, p. 32.

9. Michael Knight, "Earnhardt Ranks No. 1 Nationally," *Philadelphia Daily News*, October 6, 1980, p. 58.

10. Sam Moses, "Be Cool, Be Fast, Be Champ," *Sports Illustrated*, November 24, 1980, p. 85.

11. Benny Phillips and Ben Blake, with Dale Earnhardt, *Dale Earnhardt: Determined* (Charlotte, N.C.: UMI Publications, Inc. 1998), p. 62.

Chapter 5. The Intimidator

1. Frank Vehorn, *The Intimidator* (Asheboro, N.C.: Down Home Press, 1991), p. 48.

2. Tom Higgins, "Top Gun," *Charlotte Observer*, May 17, 1987, p. 1D.

3. Associated Press, "Earnhardt Bumps His Way to Miller High Life Crown," *Wichita Eagle-Beacon*, February 25, 1985, p. 5B.

4. Associated Press, "A 'Lucky' Earnhardt Slips Past Richmond to Snare Busch 500," *Lexington Herald-Leader*, August 26, 1985, p. 5B.

5. Tom Higgins, "Earnhardt Rides Through Wrecks to Win at Martinsville," *Charlotte Observer*, September 23, 1985, p. 1C.

6. Tom Higgins, "Richmond Wreck Leaves Friendly Competitors Not-so Friendly," *Charlotte Observer*, February 24, 1986, p. 3C.

7. Ibid.

Chapter 6. The Pass on the Grass

1. Tom Higgins, "Harsh Words Follow Earnhardt's Win at Bristol," *Charlotte Observer*, April 13, 1987, p. 1D.

2. Tom Higgins, "Earnhardt's Driving Talk of Circuit," *Charlotte Observer*, April 26, 1987 p. 1D.

3. Michael Vega, "Earnhardt Has His Competitors Reeling," *Boston Globe*, May 3, 1987, p. 82.

4. Frank Vehorn, *The Intimidator* (Asheboro, N.C.: Down Home Press, 1991), p. 157.

5. Vehorn, p. 170.

Chapter 7. A Seventh Championship

1. Benny Phillips and Ben Blake with Dale Earnhardt, *Dale Earnhardt: Determined* (Charlotte, N.C.: UMI Publications, Inc. 1998), p. 128.

2. Tom Higgins, "Kannapolis Kid Closes in on Title," *Charlotte Observer*, October 23, 1994, p. 1G.

3. Jim McLaurin, "Dale E. Double at the Rock, Earnhardt Gets 7th Cup, Equals Petty," *The State* (Columbia, S.C.), October 24, 1994, p. C1.

4. Ibid.

5. From Herald Wire Services, "Earnhardt Wins Winston Cup Title," *Miami Herald*, October 24, 1994, p. 2D.

6. Sandra McKee, "Earnhardt's 7th Title Fit for a King," *Baltimore Sun*, October 24, 1994, p. 1C.

7. Rick Houston, "Dale Earnhardt: The Road to Fame Was a Tough, Rocky One for the Intimidator but He Never Lost His Focus," *Richard Petty's Official Guide to 50 Years of NASCAR* CSM Group, Street and Smith's Sports Group and Petty Marketing Company L.L.C., 1998), p. 94.

8. Sandra McKee, "If Drivers Have Vote, It's King Dale, Not King Richard," *Baltimore Sun*, October 30, 1994, p. 1D.

9. Ibid.

10. Mark Bechtel, "The 12 Greatest Drivers: Dale Earnhardt, the Ironhead Tactics of the Man in Black Have Earned Him Throngs of Loyal Fans, a Reputation as a Tough Guy and a Record Number of Winston Cups," *Sports Illustrated Presents 50 Years of NASCAR 1948–1998*, January, 28, 1998, p. 96.

Chapter 8. A New Rival

1. Beth Tuschak, "We're All Rookies Here," *USA Today*, August 5, 1994, p. 1C.

2. Scott Fowler, "Jeff Gordon: Right on Track," *Charlotte Observer*, May 28, 1995, p. 1A.

3. Ibid.

4. Steve Crowe, "Jeff Gordon Hopes for a Repeat at Indy," *Detroit Free Press*, August 3, 1995, p. 1D.

5. Gary Long, "Reign on for Man in Black," *Miami Herald*, August 6, 1995, p. 1C.

6. Monte Dutton, "Earnhardt Puts His Own Mark on Gordon's Season: Wins 1995 Brickyard 400," *The 1995 Indianapolis Stock Cars Yearbook* (Speedway, Ind.: Carl Hughness Publishing, 1996), p. 63.

7. Jim McLaurin, "He's 'Not Dead Yet' Earnhardt Looks Slick on Brick, Cup Champ Edges Wallace at Indy," *The State* (Columbia, S.C.), August 6, 1995. p. C1.

8. Don Coble, "Dale Earnhardt has Spent Most of the Stock Car Season Waiting to Throw the Knockout Punch on 24-year-old Jeff Gordon: The Big Blow Apparently Won't Happen," *Gannett News Service*, November 11, 1995 <http://www.elibrary.com>, March 22, 2000.

9. Associated Press, "Brief Lead Gives Gordon NASCAR Series Title," *Los Angeles Times*, November 13, 1995, Sports, p. 13.

10. Steve Crowe, "Gordon: Wonder Boy Among Racing's Men," *Detroit Free Press*, November 11, 1995, p. 1B.

11. Mike Harris, Associated Press, "A Wonder Boy Is Taking Spot Among NASCAR's Elite," *Philadelphia Inquirer*, March 19, 1995, p. C7.

Chapter 9. Trouble on the Track

1. Bruce Newman, "Nasty Racing: Jeff Gordon Was Glad to Get Out of Talladega with His Sixth Win of the Season, While Dale Earnhardt Was Glad to Get Out Alive," *Sports Illustrated Presents the NASCAR 1996 Winston Cup Series*, p. 86.

2. Ibid.

3. Bruce Newman, "A Long, Rough Ride: It Was a Painful Year for Dale Earnhardt, Who Had to Endure Injury and, Worse, Losing," *Sports Illustrated Presents the NASCAR 1996 Winston Cup Series*, p. 132.

4. Ibid.

5. Dick Brinster, Associated Press, "Earnhardt Goes from Second to on His Roof Again" *The News Journal* (Wilmington, Del.), February 17, 1997, p. C4.

6. Ron Green, "Ironhead Rides Scrap Metal to Finish," *Charlotte Observer* February 16, 1997, <http://www.charlotte.com>, February 18, 1998.

7. Ed Hinton, "Asleep at the Wheel," *Sports Illustrated*, September 15, 1997, p. 88.

Chapter 10. The Future

1. Ben White, "Back on Track," *NASCAR Winston Cup Illustrated*, March 1999, p. 45.

2. Benny Phillips and Ben Blake with Dale Earnhardt, *Dale Earnhardt: Determined* (Charlotte, N.C.: UMI Publications, Inc. 1998), p. 18.

3. Ibid., p. 178.

4. White, p. 50.

5. Phillips and Blake with Earnhardt, p. 147.

Career Statistics

Season	Races Started	Wins	Top 5s	Top 10s	Poles	$ Won	Winston Cup Standings
1975	1	0	0	0	0	$1,925	n/a
1976	2	0	0	0	0	$3,085	103
1977	1	0	0	0	0	$1,375	117
1978	5	0	1	2	0	$20,145	43
1979	27	1	11	17	4	$264,086	7
1980	31	5	19	24	0	$588,926	1
1981	31	0	9	17	0	$347,113	7
1982	30	1	7	12	1	$375,325	12
1983	30	2	9	14	1	$446,272	8
1984	30	2	12	22	0	$616,788	4
1985	28	4	10	16	1	$546,596	8
1986	29	5	16	23	1	$1,783,880	1
1987	29	11	21	24	1	$2,099,243	1
1988	29	3	13	19	0	$1,214,089	3
1989	29	5	14	19	0	$1,435,730	2
1990	29	9	18	23	4	$3,083,056	1
1991	29	4	14	21	0	$2,396,685	1
1992	29	1	6	15	1	$915,463	12
1993	30	6	17	21	2	$3,353,789	1
1994	31	4	20	25	2	$3,300,733	1
1995	31	5	19	23	3	$3,154,241	2
1996	31	2	13	17	2	$2,285,926	4
1997	32	0	7	16	0	$2,151,909	5
1998	33	1	5	13	0	$2,611,100	8
1999	34	3	7	21	0	$3,048,236	7
Career Totals	641	74	268	404	23	$36,045,716	7 Winston Cup Titles

Where to Write
Dale Earnhardt

Mr. Dale Earnhardt
Dale Earnhardt, Inc.
1675 Coddle Creek Hwy.
Mooresville, NC 28115

On the Internet at:

Official NASCAR Web site
<http://www.NASCAR.com>

The Earnhardt Connection—Dale Earnhardt NASCAR News
<http://www.daleearnhardt.net/>

Index

W9-AYO-746

DISCARD

Look for these

ROTTEN SCHOOL
books, too!

The Great
Smelling Bee

The Big
Blueberry
Barf~Off!

Lose, Team, Lose!

The Good,
the Bad and
the Very Slimy

ROTTEN SCHOOL

GROWTH · LEARNING · PIZZA!

Shake, Rattle, & HURL!

R.L. STINE

Illustrations by Trip Park

HarperCollins*Publishers*

A Parachute Press Book

CHESTERFIELD COUNTY LIBRARY
VIRGINIA

For Cameron
—TP

Shake, Rattle, & Hurl!
Copyright © 2006 by Parachute Publishing, L.L.C.
Cover copyright © 2006 by Parachute Publishing, L.L.C.

All rights reserved.
No part of this book may be used or reproduced in any manner whatsoever
without written permission except in the case of brief quotations embodied in
critical articles and reviews. Printed in the United States of America.

For information address HarperCollins Children's Books, a division of
HarperCollins Publishers, 1350 Avenue of the Americas, New York, NY 10019.
www.harperchildrens.com

Library of Congress Cataloging-in-Publication Data
Stine, R. L.
    Shake, rattle, and hurl! / R.L. Stine ; illustrations by Trip Park.— 1st ed.
        p.   cm. — (Rotten School ; #5)
    "A Parachute Press Book."
    Summary: Rotten School schemer Bernie Bridges is determined that Rotten House
will beat Nyce House in the annual talent contest.
    ISBN-10: 0-06-078811-9 (trade bdg.) — ISBN-10: 0-06-078812-7 (lib. bdg.)
    ISBN-13: 978-0-06-078812-4 (lib. bdg.) — ISBN-13: 978-0-06-078811-7 (trade bdg.)
    [1. Boarding schools—Fiction. 2. Schools—Fiction. 3. Talent shows—Fiction.] I.
Park, Trip, ill. II. Title. III. Series.
PZ7.S86037She 2006   2005018355
[Fic]—dc22   CIP
                                                                   AC

Cover and interior design by mjcdesign
1 2 3 4 5 6 7 8 9 10

First Edition

— CONTENTS —

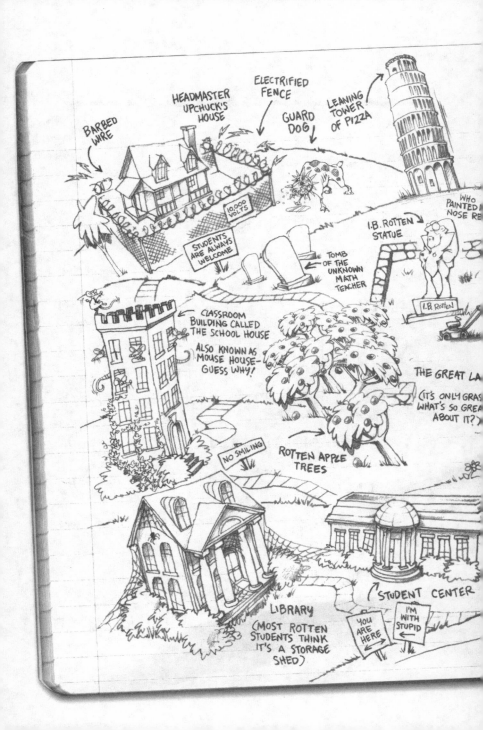

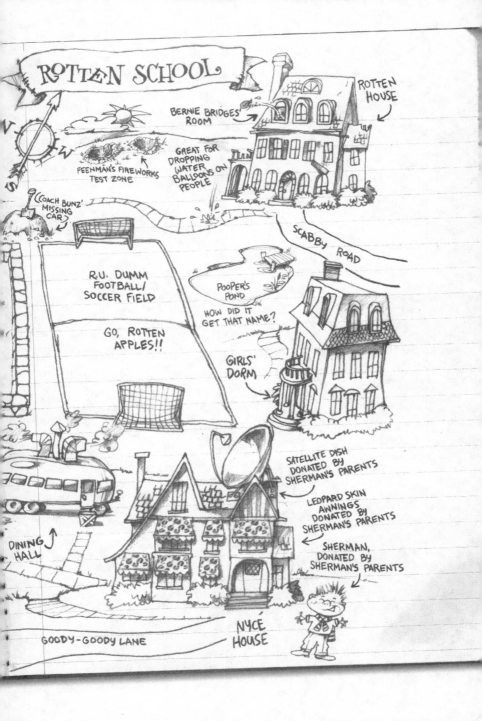

MORNING ANNOUNCEMENTS

Good morning, Rotten Students. This is Headmaster Upchuck. I hope you're all ready for another Rotten day. Here are the morning announcements. . . .

Congratulations to Eric Spindlebag, who won a national essay contest. The topic was: WHAT IT MEANS TO BE A CONCERNED CITIZEN OF OUR NATION. And Eric's essay was titled "What Do I Win?"

1

Buck Naykid, president of the Fifth-Grade Losers Club, makes this request: "Yes, we are losers. But we don't like to be called losers. We like to be called *winner-challenged*. Thank you."

Those students who insist on wearing superhero costumes to class: Please hang your capes in your lockers. And make sure your tights fit properly so we don't have any more embarrassing problems like last Tuesday.

Nurse Hanley has an important reminder to all first graders: Vaseline is *not* a food.

And here's a special dinner announcement: Chef Baloney announces that it's Endangered Species Night in the Dining Hall.

2

HOW I LOST MY LUNCH

"Yo! Looking way good today, dudes!" I said to my buddies Feenman and Crench.

"Thanks, Bernie," Feenman said.

He had yellow stains on the front of his school blazer. That meant he had eggs for breakfast.

Crench's fly was open, and the bottom of his school tie poked out.

They're both total slobs. But I like to encourage my guys. So I lie and tell them how good they look.

It's a *nice* lie, right?

They plopped their lunch trays down on the table.

"What are you eating, Bernie?" Feenman asked. He poked his nose into my plate.

"I'm on a health food kick," I said. "Pizza and French fries."

Down the table, our buddy Beast burped so hard, he rocketed off his chair. When Beast burps, big chunks fly from his mouth and sail across the room.

If you don't duck in time, it can get pretty gross.

Beast climbed back up and began pawing food into his mouth with both hands. When he finished, he had chili and spaghetti noodles all over his face and stuck in his hair. For dessert he pulled stuff out of his hair and ate it.

I'm thinking of entering Beast in the school Talent Contest next week. His talent is making everyone *sick*!

My buddies and I have our own table in the Dining Hall—the Rotten House table. See, Rotten House is the name of the dorm we live in. Actually, it's a broken-down old house. But we love it.

We live on the third floor. Which is perfect for spitting on people down below. Of course, we'd *never* do such a rude thing. We'd never even *think* about it.

You probably go home every day after school. But we don't. The Rotten School is a boarding school. We live here.

I'm Bernie Bridges. Maybe you've heard of me. I mean, word *does* get around about guys who are smart, and popular, and natural-born leaders.

I would *never* say that about myself, of course. But I've heard others say it about me.

I finished my pizza and admired my reflection in the empty plate. If only I weren't so modest! I could tell you what an awesome-looking dude I am.

I looked up and saw Beast emptying the salt and pepper shakers into his open mouth. Cool dude.

Lunch is always a fun time here in the Dining Hall. It's a huge room, with a cafeteria line at one end. And rows and rows of tables, enough for kids from all three dorms.

I started to get up to get another slice of pizza. But I stopped when I heard a sound at the front of the room.

A *honk*. And then a drumbeat. A *tweet*. Another *honk*.

I turned to the front and saw a band getting ready to play.

And that's when I nearly lost my lunch.

Chapter 2

THE PLOPPS

Which dorm do we Rotten House dudes hate the most?

Nyce House.

And there, at the front of the Dining Hall, stood the Nyce House Band, getting ready to play.

I saw my archenemy, that spoiled, rich kid Sherman Oaks. Sherman has no talent. He's *too rich* to bother with talent.

So he always stands to the side and shakes a tambourine. Sometimes, he hires a kid to shake the tambourine for him!

8

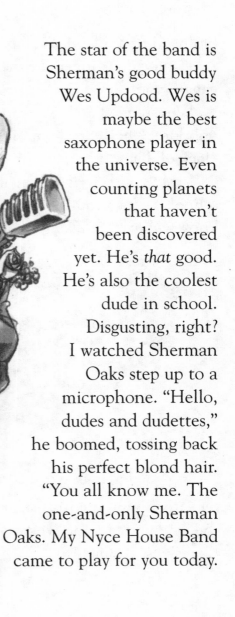

The star of the band is Sherman's good buddy Wes Updood. Wes is maybe the best saxophone player in the universe. Even counting planets that haven't been discovered yet. He's *that* good. He's also the coolest dude in school. Disgusting, right? I watched Sherman Oaks step up to a microphone. "Hello, dudes and dudettes," he boomed, tossing back his perfect blond hair. "You all know me. The one-and-only Sherman Oaks. My Nyce House Band came to play for you today.

9

No need to applaud. We know we're *way* fabulous!"

I stuck my finger down my throat and made a gagging noise.

Wes stepped up beside Sherman, carrying his saxophone. "Jack of diamonds, everyone!" he said. "Jack of diamonds, man. Silver dollars—no change!"

I told you Wes is the coolest guy in school. He's so totally cool, no one ever knows what he's *talking* about!

"Silver dollars!" Wes repeated, pumping his fist in the air. "Pudding for everyone! Blue skies, people!"

Huh? I wish I was cool enough to understand that.

Wes raised his saxophone to his mouth, and the band started to play. Kids all over the Dining Hall started to clap as music poured from Wes's sax.

His hands moved frantically over the horn. He swung it from side to side. He leaned way back and let the notes float up to the rafters. Then he ducked low, and the sounds came out like an animal growl.

As the other players kept the beat, Wes made his saxophone sing and honk and wail and cry.

I felt sick. I hated the grin on Sherman's face as he shook his tambourine, his eyes closed.

I glanced around the big room. Kids were *loving* it. My eyes stopped at the girls' table near the band. I saw April-May June rocking and bopping to the music.

April-May June, *my* girlfriend—only she doesn't know it yet. She was swaying from side to side, clapping her hands—really into it.

Oh, sick.

I had to look away. I turned to Feenman and Crench. Crench was slapping his hands to the rhythm, slapping them on Feenman's head.

"Stop it," I said. "What is the big deal here?" I had to shout over the music.

"Wes is awesome!" Feenman said, shaking his head in time to the music.

"Give me a break." I groaned. "What's so hard about playing a saxophone? You blow into it and move your fingers around. That's all there is to it."

"Wes Updood is gonna win the Talent Contest again this year," Feenman said.

I rolled my gorgeous brown eyes. "So what?"

Feenman leaned closer. "Know what the prize is? Two tickets to see The Plopps concert. *And* you get to meet them backstage."

"The Plopps?" I started to choke. Feenman had to pound me on the back. "The P-p-plopps?" I gasped.

My heart pounded. My eyeballs started rolling around in my head.

"The Plopps?" I cried, leaping to my feet. "They're my favorite band! I've downloaded every song they ever did!"

"Easy, Bernie, easy," Crench said, pulling me back into my seat.

But I couldn't calm down. "The Plopps! The Plopps!" I cried. "Have you heard their greatest hits CD? *Plopping Across America?*"

I realized I was drooling.

Crench wiped my chin for me with his blazer sleeve. "Yeah," he said. "Those two Plopp sisters are *hot*."

"I can't believe Wes Updood is gonna meet them," Feenman said. "And he'll probably take his best buddy, Sherman Oaks, to the concert with him."

"No way!" I said. I jumped to my feet again. "Rotten House has *got* to win the Talent Contest this year! I'm going to that Plopps concert. No one can stop me!"

Chapter 3

BIRD PLOP

Famous last words, right?

"Bernie, we can't win the Talent Contest," Feenman said, shaking his head.

"Yeah. We've got one little problem," Crench said.

"Problem? What problem?" I asked.

They both answered together: "We don't have any TALENT!"

I felt sick. I ate three more slices of pizza, but they didn't go down well.

I sat at the table, watching the Nyce House Band, thinking hard. Thinking about the awesome Plopp

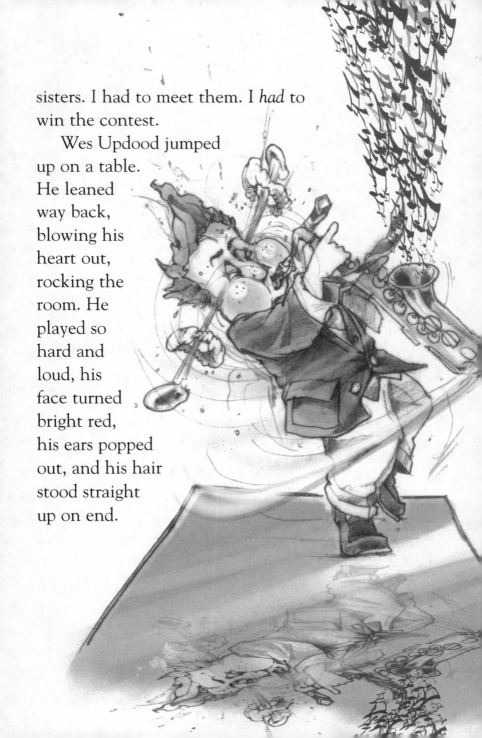

sisters. I had to meet them. I *had* to win the contest.

Wes Updood jumped up on a table. He leaned way back, blowing his heart out, rocking the room. He played so hard and loud, his face turned bright red, his ears popped out, and his hair stood straight up on end.

All the kids in the Dining Hall crowded around the table. They were clapping and shouting and dancing and rocking to the music.

Big deal, I thought.

So he's talented. It takes more than *talent* to win a talent show.

After lunch, I caught up to April-May June on the Great Lawn. It was a warm, sunny day. Butterflies fluttered over the grass. Birds twittered in the branches of the rotten apple trees.

"Hey, whussup?" I said to April-May. "I like what you did with your hair. Is that a new hair clip or something?"

"I have bird plop in my hair," she said. "I should never walk under the apple trees. I'm hurrying to my room to wash it out."

April-May always acts like she's in a hurry whenever I see her. That's because she doesn't know she's my girlfriend yet.

I had to jog to keep up with her. "April-May, can I ask you an important question?" I said.

"No," she answered. She started to run faster.

"Would you like to come see The Plopps concert

with me?" I shouted after her.

"I'm going to the concert with Wes Updood," she said. "After he wins the Talent Contest."

I tackled her around the waist to slow her down. "What if Wes doesn't win?" I said.

She tossed back her head and laughed for about five minutes. "Bernie, did you just hear Wes play? He was *awesome*! He's the most talented kid in the whole school!"

I rolled my eyes. "April-May, there's more to life than being the most talented," I said. "What about good looks?"

I pulled off my glasses and flashed her my best smile. When I smile, I have two adorable dimples in my cheeks. It's my best feature. It takes a heart of stone to ignore them.

"Take your good looks for a long walk, Bernie," April-May said.

She took off, running full speed toward the girls' dorm. Her blond hair flew behind her. The big hunk of bird plop glowed in the sunlight.

"Does that mean you'll go with me?" I shouted.

She made a rude spitting noise.

I took that for a *maybe*.

I walked off, muttering to myself. I talk to myself a lot. Who *else* understands pure genius?

"You'll see," I said. "You'll change your mind, April-May. I'm gonna win that contest. You'll see. I've got a plan...."

Chapter 4

GASSY SHOWS OFF

After dinner I hurried back to Rotten House and gathered my buddies in my room.

Feenman, Crench, and Belzer are crammed into the tiny room across the hall from me. It used to be a closet. I have my own room, about five times as big.

They insisted I take it. They wanted me to have my own room. They knew I need a lot of space for scheming and thinking and planning. And I needed space to hang my favorite poster—the life-size poster of ME!

Feenman and Crench were fighting over a bag of

potato chips. They kept snatching the bag out of each other's hands—until the bag tore open and the chips all fell to the floor.

Gassy, my big, beautiful bulldog, dove on the chips and snuffled them all up in less than ten seconds, and then licked all the salt off the floor.

Can you guess how Gassy got his name?

I turned to my friend Belzer. "Did you walk Gassy tonight?"

Belzer flashed me his crooked grin. He had taken off his school blazer. He was wearing a T-shirt with big, red letters that said: PARDON MY FRENCH.

I don't know where he finds these lame T-shirts.

"I walked Gassy," Belzer said. "Then I fed him."

"Did you taste his food first to make sure it was warm enough?" I asked.

Belzer nodded. "I ate a few spoonfuls out of the can."

Good kid, Belzer. It took a long time to train him. But it was worth it.

My three friends dropped down on the edge of my bed. "Don't wrinkle the bedspread," I said. "It's pure silk."

I pulled Gassy into the center of the room. "Okay, quiet, everyone. Quiet. I'm gonna show you the *killer* act that's gonna win the Talent Contest."

I started to feel excited. I knew I had something BIG.

"What's your act, Bernie?" Crench asked. "Card tricks or something?"

"Crench," I answered, "why would I do card tricks when I have Gassy the Great here?"

I pulled the fat bulldog to his feet. He plopped on his stomach again.

"Belzer, hold him up," I said. "You know he doesn't like to stand up on his own."

Belzer grabbed Gassy around the belly and hoisted him to his feet.

"Now watch carefully, dudes," I said. "An amazing trick. I taught Gassy how to count to one!"

"Huh?" Crench said, scratching his hair. "Bernie, *one* isn't very high."

"For a dog?" I cried. "For a dog, it's like counting to a *million*! It's taken me all week to get him to count to one. But watch. It's brilliant. It can't lose."

Belzer held the dog up. I stared Gassy in the eye.

"Go ahead, boy," I said. "Start counting!"
Gassy didn't move. Then we heard a long, loud

BRRRAAAP.

"Ohhhh!" Belzer let out a groan and let go of the dog. "He stinks! Oh, man, he STINKS! Air! Air! I need AIR!"

Feenman and Crench held their noses.

"Bernie, your act STINKS!" Feenman said.

"But that's ONE!" I exclaimed. "Don't you see? That's how he counts to one!"

BRRRAAAP.

Another loud noise from the fat bulldog.

"Is he *brilliant?*" I asked. "Is he a *genius?* He just counted to *two!*"

"I can't breathe. Air! Air!" Belzer moaned.

"Go stick your head out the window," I said.

But there was no room. Feenman and Crench already had their heads out the window.

"Okay. Okay. Forget Gassy," I said. "I've got a better act. This act will *kill!* It can't lose."

Chapter 5

THE NEW ACT IS BIG!

"Dudes, check this out," I said. I pulled Feenman and Crench back to the bed. "Sit down. Watch this."

"You've got another act, Bernie?" Belzer asked.

I nodded. "Bernie B. *always* has another act!" I said. "I'm gonna win the Talent Contest for Rotten House. Have I ever let you guys down?"

"Never!" they all cried at once.

"Am I always there for you guys?" I asked.

"Always!" they all cried at once.

"Who convinced Mrs. Heinie to give extra credit if we stay in our seats for a whole class?" Belzer asked.

"Bernie did!" Feenman and Crench cheered.

"And who convinced Chef Baloney that Gummi Worms are an important part of a healthy breakfast?" Belzer cried.

"Bernie did!" Feenman and Crench chanted.

"Hooray, Bernie!"

Belzer pumped his fists in the air. "And who convinced Headmaster Upchuck to put SpongeBob SquarePants on the Rotten School Honor Roll of Famous Living Americans?"

"Actually, Billy the Brain did that," I said.

Billy lives downstairs. He's the brainiest kid in school. But for some reason he thinks SpongeBob SquarePants is *real*.

Anyway, we all cheered, and slapped high fives, and did the secret Rotten House Handshake.

"Okay, simmer down, guys," I said. "I want to show you this new act. This one can't lose. I'm going to do impressions of all our teachers. The judges will go crazy for this."

Feenman squinted at me. "Impressions? What kind of impressions?" he asked.

"Watch," I said.

I took off my glasses and pulled on a pair of inch-thick glasses. Then I turned to Belzer. "Take the two pillows off my bed," I said. "Stuff them down the back of my jeans."

Feenman and Crench gaped at me as if I were nuts. But Belzer is trained never to ask questions. He took the pillows and jammed them down the back of my jeans.

"Okay, who am I?" I said.

They stared at me.

"I'm Mrs. Heinie," I said. "Get it?" I strutted around the room, bent forward, staring through the thick eyeglasses with my huge butt sticking out behind me.

"Get it? Look at the size of this butt! I'm Mrs. Heinie! Brilliant?"

"Uh . . . not too brilliant," Crench muttered. He and Feenman were staring over my shoulder.

I turned to the open door.

Guess who was standing there.

You got it.

Mrs. Heinie.

Chapter 6

HEINIE TROUBLE

I squinted through my thick eyeglasses—and saw Mrs. Heinie squinting back at me through *her* thick eyeglasses.

Uh-oh. Double uh-oh.

Was she smiling? No. I wouldn't describe the look on her face as a smile. I'd describe it as the look people have in a horror movie when they see the ugly, evil, man-eating monster for the first time.

Behind the glasses her eyes were bulging like tennis balls, and her mouth had dropped open to her knees.

Mrs. Heinie is our teacher and our dorm mother. And we all think she's terrific. She's not a kind person, but she's very fair.

She has a job to do as dorm mother. And that job is to keep us from being us. In other words, she has to make sure that we don't have *too much* fun.

It's a tough job. And despite the fact that she's a little nearsighted and a little bent over, she's a tough woman.

And now here she was in the doorway to my room, watching me strut around, doing my two-pillow impression of her.

Most kids would fall to the floor and start to cry and plead insanity.

But not Bernie Bridges. Do you think I can't talk my way out of anything?

"Yo, Mrs. Heinie," I greeted her with my most

adorable, dimpled smile. "Would you like to join our game?"

She made a choking sound. Her bulging eyes were locked on my huge butt. "Game?"

"Yes, we're having such awesome fun," I said, keeping the dimples flashing. "We're playing Pillow Search. It's a totally popular game. Everyone in the dorm is playing it."

Mrs. Heinie made another choking sound. "Popular?" she said.

"You're looking lovely tonight, Mrs. H.," I said. "I see you are dressed up. Are you going to a fancy party? I *know* you. I know you have a secret party life we boys don't know about."

"Bernie, I'm wearing my bathrobe," she said. She frowned at me. "Let's get back to the game."

"Oh, yes," I said. "The game. See? The rules are pretty simple. We take turns hiding the pillow. Then everyone tackles the guy with the pillow."

I turned to Feenman, Crench, and Belzer. "Okay. Tackle me, guys. Go ahead. Tackle me. Show Mrs. H. how the game works.

My three friends didn't move. They sat hunched

on the bed, paralyzed, staring at me with their mouths hanging open.

"Ha-ha." I laughed. "They're a little shy. But it's a great game. We play it all the time."

Mrs. Heinie didn't move. She just stared at me, frowning, her face wrinkled up tight like a very pale prune.

"Uh...are you buying this story?" I asked.

She rolled her eyes. "What do *you* think?"

I swallowed noisily. "So...I'm in major trouble?"

She nodded. "Yes. Major trouble." She spun around and started to leave. But then she stuck her head back in the door. "You know, Bernie," she said, "*one* pillow would have been enough!"

Chapter 7

KIDNAPPED!

We waited for Mrs. Heinie to go up the stairs to her apartment in the attic. Then we all fell on the floor laughing. Feenman pulled the pillows from my pants, and we had a big pillow fight. Just letting off some steam.

Finally, I got everyone quiet. "Dudes, we still need an act for the Talent Contest," I said. "Hey, I've got another idea."

I pulled a bunch of toilet paper rolls out from a desk drawer. I'm not sure why I was saving them. I knew they'd come in handy one day.

I handed each guy a toilet paper roll. "We'll hum into them," I said. "We'll totally rock. Come on, dudes. Let's work up some awesome harmony. We'll play better than Wes's band."

I hummed a rock riff into my toilet paper roll.

Feenman made a disgusted face. "Sorry, Big B," he said. "That idea totally *wipes*."

I think he was making a joke. But he was right.

I slapped myself on the forehead. "Come on, Bernie. Think. *Think* of something!"

I *had* to come up with an act to beat Wes Updood.

"Hey, I'm going out, guys," I said. "I'm gonna take a walk. Sometimes fresh air helps me think."

They didn't hear me. They were singing into their toilet paper rolls at the top of their lungs.

I hurried downstairs and stepped out the front door. It was a clear, warm night. An owl hooted high in a nearby tree.

I took a deep breath and inhaled the strong aroma from the rotten apple trees on the Great Lawn. Mmmmm. Nothing like that smell to wake up your brain.

Sometimes I head over to Pooper's Pond to stare at the water and think. Don't ask me how the pond got that name. No one seems to know.

I turned and started to follow the narrow path to the pond.

And who was the first kid I ran into? Wes Updood. Carrying his saxophone case at his side.

"What's up, Wes?" I said. "You going to band practice?"

"Marshmallow Fluff, dude," he replied. "It's like Custer's Last Stand. Know what I mean? Extra creamy, with half the carbs."

"Cool," I said. I kept walking.

I was almost to the pond when strong hands grabbed me around the waist and spun me around.

I stared into the chunky, panting face of *Jennifer Ecch!*

I call her Nightmare Girl. That's because she's twice as big as I am, twice as strong—and totally in love with me.

A nightmare.

Do you know how *embarrassing* it is to be in fourth grade and have a girl who follows you around making loud smoochy noises and calling you "Honey Lips" and "Butter Cakes"?

It totally *wipes*!

"Hurry," she whispered. She picked me up off the ground.

"No!" I cried. "Jennifer—don't touch me. I have a flesh-eating disease. You don't want to catch it. It'll eat *your* flesh, too!"

She ignored me. She hoisted me over her broad shoulders and started to jog across the grass.

"Where are you taking me?" I cried, bouncing on her shoulder. "What are you doing?"

"Shhh. Quiet, Honey Face," she said. "Come with me. We're gonna win the Talent Contest!"

Chapter 8

WHO'S THE DUMMY?

Jennifer carried me into the girls' dorm. I heard girls giggling as she trotted down the front hall.

Finally, she set me down in the Commons Room. Every dorm has a Commons Room. It's like a big living room for everyone living in the dorm. You know. Couches and big armchairs, a TV, a game table.

I glanced around. We were the only ones there.

"Jennifer, I have to get back to my dorm," I said, glancing at the clock over the mantel. "I'm already in trouble with Mrs. Heinie. I can't—"

"Shut up, Sweet Breath," she said. She grabbed

my arm and yanked me across the room to a big, red armchair. "I heard you love The Plopps. Do you want to go to their concert or not?"

"Of course, I do," I said. "But—"

"Well, I know how we can do it," Jennifer said. She blew the hair from her eyes. She does that all the time. It's a habit, I guess. But I really hate it when she blows the hair from *my* eyes!

"How can we win the Talent Contest?" I asked. "Do you have a secret talent?"

"Of *course!*" she answered.

This was starting to get interesting.

I know. I know. I usually do *anything* to keep away from Jennifer Ecch. I once jumped in Pooper's Pond and stayed underwater for three minutes to keep her from seeing me.

That's pretty gross—right?

But tonight I was desperate. Desperate to beat Sherman and Wes and Nyce House. And desperate to see The Plopps.

"What's your talent?" I asked The Ecch. "Do you *eat* an entire car?"

"Don't be stupid, Sweet Ears," Jennifer said. "I'm

a great ventriloquist. I can throw my voice."

I stared at her. First at her blue eye, then at her brown eye. "No joke?"

"I just threw my voice," she said. "Could you hear it?"

"No," I replied.

"That's because I threw it really far," she said. She blew the hair out of her eyes again. "Listen, Bernie, we can do an awesome act together and win the big prize."

"I don't get it," I said. "Why do you need me?"

"I don't have a dummy," Jennifer said. "I can't do a ventriloquist act without a dummy. So . . . you're *it*."

"Huh? No *way*!" I cried.

She grinned. "You *love* the idea—don't you! I can tell. It'll be a *riot*, Honey Knees."

"PLEEEASE don't call me Honey Knees!" I begged.

"How can we lose?" Jennifer said.

She grabbed me and pulled me down onto her lap on the chair.

"This act is gonna be way wicked," she said.

"There's never been a ventriloquist act like this."
She slid her arms around my waist. I felt her hot
breath on the back of my neck.

"Okay," I said. "Let's start."

Hello, I just LOVE Honey Face!

I waited for her to throw her voice. Or tell a joke. Or ask me a question or something.

I waited. And waited.

And waited.

"Uh . . . Jennifer?" I said.

She grabbed my hand. Squeezed it in both of hers. And started planting smoochy kisses all over it.

"Uh . . . Jen," I said quietly, "you're not a ventriloquist—are you?"

Smooch. Smooch. Smooch.

My hand was sopping wet.

"Uh . . . well . . . no." She finally answered my question.

"You can't throw your voice—can you?" I asked.

Smooch smooch.

"No, Lovey Chin. Actually, I can't."

I sighed. "And this was just an excuse to get me to sit in your lap, *wasn't* it!" I exclaimed.

"Yes," she said.

Chapter 9

BABOOM
BABOOM

The next afternoon I ran into Sherman Oaks outside the School House, our classroom building. He flashed me his perfect, 65-toothed smile. "Guess where I'm coming from, Bernie."

"Having your head bronzed?" I said.

"No. Headmaster Upchuck's office. We were practicing." Sherman smiled again, an even brighter smile. So bright, I had to shield my eyes.

"I envy you," I said. "Headmaster Upchuck is a man among men. He's a man I look up to. Well, yes, he's only three feet tall. I guess I can't really look *up* to him. But what does that matter? The man is a GIANT. He—"

Sherman rolled his eyes. "Bernie, aren't you going to ask me what we were practicing in his office?"

"Okay," I said. "What were you practicing?"

"Him handing me the First Prize trophy for winning the Talent Contest," Sherman said.

"Excuse me?" *Gulp.* I swallowed my bubble gum. "You—you—"

"The Headmaster likes to get it right," Sherman said. "You know. When he comes onstage at the end to give the trophy to the winner? He wants the handoff to be smooth. So he and I practiced it for about an hour."

I took a deep breath. "But he handed it to the wrong guy, Sherman," I said.

"Because you're not going to win. I am!"

Sherman tossed back his head, opened his mouth wide, and laughed for about ten minutes. He laughed until he got the hiccups.

Then, wiping the tears from his eyes, he took my arm. "Come here, Bernie—*HIC*. Let me show you—*HIC*—one more reason you're not going to win."

He dragged me into Nyce House, his dorm. I instantly started to shake and sweat. The place gives me the deep creeps. It's clean and neat and quiet.

Who would *live* in a place like that?

As we passed the front hall I saw the dorm parents, Sam and Janet Pocketlint. They wore matching school uniforms and carried matching dust mops.

They were dusting everything in sight.

Gross.

Sherman pulled me into his room. I nearly gagged. The bed was made!

He had a furry, white sheepskin bedspread, and a sheepskin rug covered his floor. He had a wide-screen TV on his dresser. A music system with huge floor speakers that nearly reached the ceiling. On the wall above his bed he had a big, green-and-black poster of a *dollar sign*.

"Check this out," Sherman said. He dragged me to a large keyboard standing against the wall. "This is my new digital drum machine," he said.

I was still shaking and sweating. But I pulled myself together. "Very nice, Shermy," I said, slapping him on the back. "And what do you plan to do with it? Annoy your neighbors?"

"No," he said. "My parents bought it for me so I can play drums in Wes Updood's band." He glanced at the big dollar sign on the wall. "It cost five thousand dollars. But my parents really want to buy my love."

"But you don't know *how* to play drums," I said.

He sneered. "What does *that* matter?" He clicked the power switch on. A soft rhythm started. He turned up the volume.

"See? You pick any rhythm," he said. "Then you pick a speed. Here."

He turned a knob. I heard

BOOM BABOOM BABOOM BOOM.

"There it goes," Sherman said. "Sweet, huh? It's perfect for the band's first number."

"But what do *you* do?" I asked.

Sherman squinted at me. "Me? I don't do anything. It's all digital. It plays itself. I'm too rich. Why work up a sweat?"

"Can I try it?" I asked. "Hmm. Let me see . . ."

I grabbed the volume knob. "Is this the rhythm knob?"

I turned it up all the way.

BOOM BABOOOM BABOOOOM BOOOOM

A deafening roar blasted from the machine. Two windows broke.

Sherman covered his ears. "Turn it down!" he shrieked. "Bernie! The volume! Turn it DOWN!"

I pretended I couldn't find the volume. "Which knob is it?" I screamed. "Is it this one? No. How about this one? No. Sorry, Sherman. I'm just not good with these digital things."

I pulled the volume knob off and held it in the air. "Is this it? I think it's broken."

BOOM
BABOOOM
BABOOOOM
BOOOOM

The walls were shaking. I saw a big crack split the ceiling. The sheepskins were jumping as if they had come alive!

Sherman fell to his knees, covering his ears, wailing in agony.

It was *way* painful.

I took off running. The throbbing, electronic drumbeats were shaking the whole house.

I was nearly out the front door. But I stopped at the entrance to the Commons Room.

"Whoa." I saw April-May June. She was sitting on a couch beside Wes Updood.

What's up with that?

He was playing his saxophone. Showing off. He was making it honk like a duck and making it do gross, rude noises.

And April-May was slapping her knees, tossing back her blond hair, laughing her head off. She thought Wes was a riot.

"She doesn't *really* like Wes Updood," I growled to myself. "She likes *me*. She just doesn't know it yet. When Rotten House wins the Talent Contest, she'll be *begging* me to take her to The Plopps concert."

The honking stopped. Wes saw me in the doorway. He waved.

"Instant pancakes, dude!" he called to me. "Yo, Bernie—instant pancakes, man! Nothing but the best. Know what I'm saying?"

"Yeah. Instant pancakes," I replied. And I hurried out the door.

Chapter 10

"Ow!"

Belzer, Feenman, and Crench jammed into my room after dinner. They seemed very excited. All three of them were talking at once.

"We've got it, Big B!"

"We're gonna win."

"We've got the act. We've got it!"

"Well, it's about time," I said, jumping up from my computer. "I knew my guys would come through. You found a fabulously talented dude hiding in the dorm?"

"Not exactly," Belzer said.

"Belzer, did you have spinach at dinner?" I asked.

"Well, yeah," he replied. "How'd you know?"

"You've got big, green globs of spinach stuck to your braces."

"No problem, Big B," he said. "It always dissolves in two or three days."

Feenman pulled me away from Belzer. "Bernie, forget the spinach. You've gotta see our act. We're the *best*!"

"*Your* act?" I took a few steps back. "You three? What kind of an act? Guess what, guys? Eating a double cheeseburger without chewing is *not* a talent!"

"We've got a better act than that," Crench said. "You ever see those old comedies on TV? The black-and-white ones with those three nutty weirdos?"

"*The Three Stooges?*" I asked.

"Yeah," Crench said. "Those dudes who are always slapping each other, hitting and kicking, and poking each other's eyes out. They're cool, right?"

"So guess what we decided to do?" Belzer said, picking long strings of spinach from between his teeth.

I stared at my friends. I counted them. One, two, three. "You guys are going to do a *Three Stooges* act?" I said.

"Wow. How did you guess that?" Feenman asked.

"Check out the act, Bernie," Crench said. "We're not just funny. We're a *riot*. The judges at the Talent Contest will fall down. Really. Forget Wes Updood. We've got it won! Watch!"

Belzer disappeared into their room across the hall for a minute. He came back carrying a baseball bat. "Okay. Ready, guys?" he asked.

"Here goes, Bernie," Crench said. "Get ready to laugh."

"I'm ready," I said. "Go ahead. Be funny."

They started their act.

"Hey, you—!" Feenman said to Crench.

"Don't say *hey*," Crench said.

"I'll say whatever I want," Feenman said. He slapped Crench's face.

Crench raised his hand to slap Feenman. Feenman ducked, and Crench slapped Belzer instead.

"Hey! What did I do?" Belzer shouted. He punched Crench in the stomach.

Crench doubled over.

"Owwww."

Feenman poked Belzer in the eyes.

"Owwwww."

Belzer punched Feenman in the chest. The punches and slaps flew. Crench slammed the baseball bat into Belzer's stomach.

"Owwww!"

"That really hurt!"

"Ohhhhh. I'm bleeding. I'm bleeding!"

"You poked my eyes out! I can't see! You poked my eyes out!"

"Owwwww."

"Help me!"

"It hurts! It hurts!"

"My head hurts! I can't see!"

I started to laugh. "Good work, dudes!" I said.

"That's a riot! That's totally funny!" I laughed some more.

They were rolling on the floor, moaning, holding their heads and their stomachs.

"Not ... funny," Belzer groaned. "Bernie, we're in pain. We're not faking it. We really *destroyed* each other!"

"I think I got a concussion," Feenman wailed.

"My ... head," Crench moaned. "It feels like my skull is fractured!"

I stopped laughing. "Guys, guys—get up!" I tried to pull them to their feet. But they were doubled over in pain.

"You know," I told them, "I don't think the Three Stooges really injured themselves in those old movies. I think they kinda *faked* it."

"You ... think ... so?" Crench groaned, holding his stomach.

"They *faked* it?" Feenman said, hands covering his eyes.

"Yeah. They didn't really punch each other and poke out each other's eyes. They just pretended," I said. "You guys have to work on the *pretending* part.

I think you need more practice."

Crench groaned. "Why didn't someone *tell* us they faked it?"

They couldn't stand up. So I rolled them out into the hall. Then I closed my bedroom door.

"What am I gonna do?" I asked myself. "The rehearsal for the Talent Contest is tomorrow night. And I've got nothing. *Nothing.*"

I have to search the dorm from top to bottom, I decided.

There *has* to be someone in Rotten House with some talent.

I decided to search every room on every floor.

I opened my door and walked into the hall. I had to step over Belzer, Feenman, and Crench to get to the stairs.

I made my way down to the second floor—and stopped.

I froze. My ears stood up on end. My heart started to pound.

"Whoa!" I cried. "What is THAT?!"

Chapter 11

THE GREATEST ROCK GUITAR EVER!

I grabbed the banister and listened. Where was that music coming from?

I held my breath. The music was *awesome*. Rock-and-roll guitar. Wailing, soaring, *rocking* sounds.

It's a CD, I decided.

One of the guys is playing a CD of a totally great guitar player.

But no. The music stopped for a moment. Then started up again, playing the same song, only in a different rhythm.

My fingers were snapping in time to the beat. I

didn't even realize it. My legs were moving. My knees were dipping. I was DANCING!

I couldn't help it. The guitar totally *kicked*!

I'd never heard rock-and-roll guitar like that *in my life*!

Now, I gripped the banister with both hands. Sweat poured down my broad, handsome forehead. My heart was doing a rock-and-roll beat in my chest!

"Someone in this dorm can play *awesome* guitar," I told myself. "I've gotta find him. I *need* him! He's gonna win the Talent Contest for me!"

I jumped off the stairs and into the second-floor hallway. Down at the far end of the hall, a bunch of second graders were laughing and shrieking, pulling down one another's jeans. They have de-pantsing contests just about every night.

They're *so* immature.

I grabbed the doorknob on the first door I came to, and pushed open the door.

My friend Nosebleed was sitting at his desk, staring at a blank sheet of paper. "What are you doing?" I asked him.

He shrugged. "I don't know. Just staring. It helps me think."

"Think about what?" I asked.

He shrugged again. "I don't know."

"Were you playing that rock guitar?" I asked him.

He shook his head. "No way. I can't play a musical instrument. It gives me a nosebleed."

I slammed his door and hurried to the next room. Down the hall, the second graders were all dancing around in their underpants.

I pulled open the next door and saw Billy the Brain sitting at his desk.

Billy has a solid C-minus average. Incredible, right? He's the smartest kid in school.

"Who's there?" Billy called. He was sitting at his desk, doing his homework *blindfolded*.

"It's me. Bernie," I said. "Why are you blindfolded?"

"To make it harder," Billy said. "I read all of my textbooks blindfolded so I won't have an unfair advantage over the rest of you dumber guys."

What a brain!

"Were you just playing guitar?" I asked him.

"I don't play guitar," Billy said. "But sometimes I

play the piano blindfolded."

I *told* you he's brilliant!

I slammed his door and hurried down the hall. I took the stairs two at a time to the second floor.

I could hear the rock guitar even louder now. Twanging, swooping, *rocking*!

Where was it coming from?

I stopped outside Chipmunk's door. The music grew louder. Was it possible?

Chipmunk is the shyest kid in school. He's so shy, he inhales when he *burps*!

I like to help my guys. I've been working with Chipmunk. Trying to get him over his shyness. But so far, even Bernie B. has failed.

"It can't be Chipmunk playing this awesome guitar," I muttered. "No way."

I pressed my ear to the door.

Yes! The music was definitely coming from inside.

I pushed open the door. "Chipmunk?" I called. "Is that *you* playing?"

My eyes searched the room. No one there.

"Chipmunk?"

Where *was* he?

Chapter 12

A STAR IS BORN

I stepped into the room. The rocking guitar swooped and soared and twanged. "Chipmunk?" I called.

I followed my ears—to the closet. I pulled open the closet door. "Yo—Chipmunk!" I cried.

He sat on a pile of dirty shirts and pants, a shiny, new guitar in his hands.

"Hi, Bernie," he said, blushing. He blushes whenever he talks.

I stared down at him. "Chipmunk—were you playing that *awesome* guitar?"

He blushed some more. "I'll stop if you want me

to," he said, lowering his eyes.

"Huh? Stop?" I cried. "You don't understand. You've gotta keep playing."

"I—I do?" he stammered, gripping the guitar in both hands.

"Why are you in the closet?" I asked.

"I don't want to bother anyone," Chipmunk replied, his eyes still down.

"Don't you realize?" I shouted. "Don't you realize you play the wickedest rock guitar I ever heard!"

He shrugged. "I practice a lot," he whispered. "I think I'm getting better." He blushed again.

I grabbed him with both hands and tugged him out of the closet. "You're gonna be a winner, Chipmunk!"

He blinked. "I am?"

"You want to get over your shyness, right? Right," I answered for him. "Well, this is your big chance."

He started to shake. "What do I have to do?" he asked in a trembling voice.

I slapped him on the back. "Play guitar, that's all," I said. "You're going to play at the Talent Contest rehearsal tomorrow after school. You're gonna be our talent."

"I—I am?" He squeezed his guitar so hard, his hands turned red.

"Chipmunk, you *rock,* dude! No way you can lose," I told him. "Everyone will fall on the floor and beg you to play some more. You'll kill! *Kill!*"

Chipmunk swallowed a few times. His big Adam's apple slid up and down. "But—but—" he sputtered.

"No buts," I said. "You've already *won.*" I started for the door. "I'm gonna bring all the guys downstairs to hear you play."

"But, but—Bernie—"

"Don't move," I said. "The guys have got to hear you *rock out!*"

I ran upstairs. No. Actually, I *flew* upstairs.

I rounded up everyone—Feenman, Crench, Belzer, Nosebleed, Billy the Brain, Farley Mopes, Beast, and a bunch of other dudes. I led them all down to Chipmunk's room.

"You're gonna fall to the ground!" I told them. "You're gonna rock till you drop! This is totally amazing!"

I pushed open Chipmunk's door, and we all rushed inside.

"Chipmunk?"

He was gone.

Chapter 13

HELP FROM A WATER BOTTLE

I glanced all around. "Where is he? Where is he? He couldn't have gone far! Find him!"

We scrambled all over the room. I pulled open the closet door. No sign of him. I tossed out the pile of dirty clothes. No. He wasn't hiding under them.

We looked everywhere—even in the dresser drawers.

Finally, Feenman found him hiding under the bed. "What are you doing under there?" he asked.

"Uh ... I do this sometimes," Chipmunk replied. "It's, um, nice under here."

"It's nice out here, too," I said. "Come out and play."

Feenman and Crench grabbed his arms and legs and pulled him out. I handed him his guitar. "Play," I said. "The guys can't wait to hear you."

He swallowed a few more times.

"Play," I said. "Rock-and-roll forever—right?"

"I guess," he muttered. He carried his guitar into the closet and closed the door behind him.

"Bernie," Feenman said, "what's with the closet?"

"Just shut up and listen," I said. "The dude is an artist. He can play wherever he wants."

A few seconds later, Chipmunk started playing. The guitar totally *rocked*!

Chipmunk's playing had a pounding beat. It was bluesy and hard-driving and wailing. It sounded like there were FIVE guitar players in that closet.

I turned to my guys. They were dancing along to the guitar music. Waving their hands high above their heads. Rocking and bopping.

"I . . . I can't believe it! Chipmunk is *talented*!" Belzer shouted.

"I told you," I said.

"Rotten House is gonna win the contest!" Crench

exclaimed. "No *way* we can lose now!"

I grinned. "Know what, dudes?" I said. "I'm gonna make sure we don't lose."

"Uh-oh," Crench said. "What are you going to do, Bernie?"

My grin grew wider. "I'm going to pay a visit to Nyce House and help Chipmunk out a little."

"You're going into Nyce House?" Feenman asked. "Bernie, you know you start to shake and sweat when you go there."

"Help Chipmunk? What do you mean?" Belzer asked.

I held up a water bottle. "I'm going to sneak into their dorm and water Wes Updood's saxophone," I said. "You know. Fill it up a little."

I pointed to the closet. "A little help for my best buddy Chipmunk, who is going to take me to The Plopps concert."

Crench stared at the water bottle. Then he frowned at me. "But, Bernie—isn't that *cheating?*"

I clapped my hand over Crench's mouth. "Cheating? Don't *ever* say that word," I told him. "It's not cheating. It's *helping!*"

Chapter 14

NOT NICE IN NYCE HOUSE

A bright full moon glowed down on me as I crept across the campus to the Nyce House dorm. I had the water bottle hidden deep in my backpack.

I kept smiling as I pictured Wes Updood stepping onstage tomorrow after school. He raises his golden saxophone to his lips. He starts to play...

And instead of musical notes, we hear *GURGLE GURGLE GURGLE*.

Yes, Bernie B. was about to play a very mean trick.

But, come on. Isn't *Talent Contest* another word for *WAR*?

I started to shake and sweat as I let myself into Nyce House through the front door. But I didn't care. I was on a mission. A mission to help my buddy Chipmunk.

The front hall was empty. The wood floors gleamed brighter than the moonlight. Sam and Janet Pocketlint must polish them every day.

In Rotten House we've never even *seen* the floor! It's too cluttered with all our junk.

I crept toward the back. I passed three big posters on the wall. In Rotten House we have NASCAR posters in the front hall. And a couple of football posters.

In Nyce House they have posters of *angels* on the wall. Old-fashioned paintings of women floating in the clouds, with big, white wings and halos over their heads.

Well, they don't call it *Nyce* House for nothing! I guess Sam and Janet Pocketlint want all their boys to act like angels.

I heard voices in the Commons Room. I stopped at the doorway and peeked in.

Sherman Oaks was in there. And Wes Updood.

And a bunch of other Nyce House guys. Sherman was showing off his drum machine.

"If I push this button, I can get a Latin rhythm," Sherman was saying. He pushed a button, and a tango-type beat started up.

"If I push this button, it sounds like cymbals crashing," Sherman said. He pushed the button, and cymbals crashed.

"You have to be a *great* musician to push the right buttons," Sherman said.

Yeah. Right.

I was happy. Sherman and Wes were busy here. That meant that Wes's room was empty. That would make it a lot easier to sneak in, fill the sax with water, and sneak back out.

Wes's room was just around the corner. I slid the backpack around to the front so I could grab the water bottle.

I was shaking and sweating. My heart started to pound out a Latin rhythm.

I stepped up to Wes's door—and someone grabbed me from behind.

Chapter 15

THE MUSIC LOVER

I spun around—and stared in horror at Sam and Janet Pocketlint!

"H-h-h-hi!" I stammered. I wanted to faint. But Bernie B. never panics. I got it together fast and flashed them my best dimpled smile. "Nice to see you!"

Mr. Pocketlint wore his school blazer and tie and baggy, khaki pants. His wife wore a black, pleated dress, down to her ankles.

He has a slender, pink face, a very long, pointed nose, and tiny blue eyes, very close together. He looks a lot like one of those anteaters you see in cartoons.

Mrs. Pocketlint has gray hair, held in place with a headband. Round, gray eyes, and a large nose that always seems to be sniffing the air.

"Young man, what are you doing here?" Mr. Pocketlint demanded.

I kept the grin on my face. I know no one can resist my adorable dimples. "Well...you see..."

Mrs. Pocketlint sniffed the air and squinted at me. "Aren't you Bernie Bridges? We've heard a lot about you."

"Lies! All lies!" I said. "People who are jealous make up lies about me."

"Well, we try to keep the riffraff out of Nyce House. What are you doing here?" Mr. Pocketlint asked again.

"Uh ... Wes Updood asked me to get his saxophone for him," I said.

They both stared at me. Mr. Pocketlint blinked his tiny, anteater eyes. "Oh, I see," he said. "You're interested in music? Do you like Mozart?"

"I play sonatas on the harpsichord," Mrs. Pocketlint said. When she smiled, her pink gums showed. She had two rows of tiny, pointed teeth.

"My left hand is very good," she continued. "But my right hand is only fair."

She smiled her gummy smile at her husband. "Sam plays the ocarina," she said, squeezing his arm.

"Come. Listen to some Mozart," Mr. Pocketlint said. "We heard you were a scheming, fast-talking, troublemaking brat. We didn't know you were a music lover."

"For sure," I said. "I love music. I *live* for music. And of course Mozart is one of my fav's. But if I could just get that saxophone ... "

They each grabbed one of my arms. "That can wait," Mrs. Pocketlint said. "First Mozart."

"But—but—"

They dragged me into a large room at the end of the hall and locked the door behind me. I saw a grand piano, a harpsichord, two music stands, and a couch. The walls had shelves and shelves of old record albums and CDs.

"This is our music room," Mr. Pocketlint said. He picked up his ocarina. It looked like a white plastic potato. He pointed with it. "Sit over there."

"But I really need to—"

Mrs. Pocketlint sat down at the piano. She sniffed the air and arranged her music in front of her. "Sam and I will start out with some familiar sonatas," she said. "I'm sure you know them."

"Which one is your favorite?" her husband asked.

"Well . . ." I swallowed. "I guess I like them all," I said.

"Then we'll play them all!" Mrs. Pocketlint exclaimed. She lowered her hands and began banging away on the piano. Mr. Pocketlint closed his tiny eyes, raised the little flute-thing to his mouth, and began to blow.

I settled back on the couch and kept a smile frozen on my face. I tried hard to keep my eyes open, but it was a struggle.

They played for hours and

hours—maybe *days*! I took a short, two-hour nap, but I don't think they noticed.

When they finally finished, they were both red-faced, panting hard, and bathed in sweat.

I jumped to my feet. My chance to escape!

"Thank you. Thank you both. That was wonderful!" I said. I clapped them both on the back and shook their hands. "I have tears in my eyes. Tears! Mozart always makes me so emotional!"

Mrs. Pocketlint flashed me her gummy smile. "What a delightful young man!"

Mr. Pocketlint smiled, too. "We'll invite you back for our eight-hour Brahms festival," he said.

"Only eight hours?" I said. "That isn't enough!"

And I took off, running. I ran down the hall. My ears were ringing from hours of Mozart. And my legs were trembling and weak.

But I still had a mission to accomplish. I still had to sneak into Wes Updood's room and pour water—

Uh-oh.

Where was that music coming from? It sounded like saxophone music.

I followed it to the Commons Room. And there was Wes, head tilted back, on his knees, swinging the sax back and forth as he played.

I failed. Bernie B. failed his friend Chipmunk. Head down, I slunk back to the dorm.

Back in Rotten House, I kissed the dirty floor.

Feenman and Crench were waiting for me in my room.

"Did you do it, Big B?" Crench asked. "Did you give Wes's saxophone the water treatment?"

"I changed my mind," I said. "We have to win this fair and square."

Feenman felt my forehead. "Fair and square? Are you *sick?*"

"We don't need dirty tricks," I said. "Listen to that awesome guitar music floating up from Chipmunk's closet. He's *awesome!* We can't lose!"

But then, a funny thing happened at the rehearsal....

Chapter 16

WHY I SAT ON CHIPMUNK

The next day, after classes, I hurried to the auditorium in the Student Center. The rehearsal was just starting. Mrs. Twinkler, the Drama teacher, was calling for the first act to come onstage.

"Bright faces, people!" she called. "Bright faces! I want to see everyone glow and shine!"

That's the way she talks. She's very cheery and enthusiastic. She's a real Twinkler.

Kids were scattered all over the auditorium. They had come to watch the auditions.

I hurried backstage to see if Chipmunk was ready.

I saw Flora and Fauna—the Peevish twins—practicing a song near the stage door. Jennifer Ecch waved to me and threw me a kiss. Sherman and Wes and their band were taking their instruments from their cases.

Where was Chipmunk?

Before I could ask anyone, Feenman and Crench came running up to me.

"Where's Chipmunk?" I asked. "The auditions are starting."

"He won't leave his room," Crench said breathlessly. "We tried, Bernie. He said he won't come out."

"He chained himself to the bed," Feenman said. "What should we do?"

"What should you do? *Unchain him!*" I cried. "What's he trying to do? Totally mess me up? How is he going to take me to The Plopps concert if he's chained to his bed?"

"Okay, Bernie," Feenman said. "We'll try again, but—"

"Tell him he's a star," I said. "Tell him he's already won. Tell him there's a million dollars for him here. In cash! Tell him *anything*! Just get him here!"

They both saluted and ran off.

I let out a long sigh and dropped into a seat in the front row.

"Glow and shine, people!" Mrs. Twinkler bubbled. "Big smiles now. We're *all* stars, remember!"

Jennifer Ecch came onstage first. She sat down on a tall stool. She had a little ventriloquist's dummy in her hands.

"Oh, noooo." I let out a loud groan when I saw the dummy clearly. It looked just like *me*!

Jennifer began her ventriloquist act. "This is Bernie," she said. "Say hello, Bernie." She made the dummy say hello in a tiny, squeaky voice. Then she made loud, smoochy noises and had the dummy kiss her back. "Bernie likes to kiss—don't you, Bernie?" she said.

Kids in the auditorium were laughing their heads off. I sank as low in my seat as I could go. Could *anything* be more embarrassing?

Flora and Fauna came on next. "We're going to sing a duet," Flora said. "The song is called 'Getting to Know You.'"

"Wonderful!" Mrs. Twinkler cried. "Sing it like you feel it!"

The Peevish twins started to sing. They didn't have good voices. They kinda sounded like cows caught in a wire fence. But it went pretty well until Fauna messed up the words.

Her sister stopped singing. "You jerk!" she cried. "You messed it up."

"I didn't mess it up—*you* did!" Fauna screamed.

"You did!"

They started slapping and punching each other. Mrs. Twinkler had to drag them off the stage.

"Losers," I muttered to myself. *No way* they can beat Chipmunk.

I glanced to the back of the auditorium. And saw Feenman and Crench dragging Chipmunk down the aisle.

I jumped to my feet. "Here he is! Our star is here! You've already won, dude!"

His whole body was trembling. His teeth chattered, and his eyes rolled in his head.

I put a hand on his shaking shoulder. "What's the problem?" I asked.

"I—I—I want my mommy!" Chipmunk said. Then he bit his tongue, so he couldn't say any more.

I turned to Feenman and Crench. "Where's his guitar?"

Feenman slapped his forehead. "Uh-oh. We forgot it."

"GO GET IT!" I screamed. "How do you expect Chipmunk to be a star without his guitar?"

They turned and took off running—again.

Chipmunk tried to run. But I tackled him, held him down on the floor, and sat on him. No way he'd escape from Bernie B.

Onstage, Wes and his band started to play. Wes leaned way back, raised his sax, and sent a beautiful melody floating over the auditorium. Kids started to clap and cheer.

I heard a loud buzz. And saw two white bolts of electricity shoot out of Sherman's drum machine. Sherman let out a shriek—and jumped about two feet in the air.

The drum machine shorted out!

"This will ruin it for these guys," I muttered.

But no. Wes kept right on rocking.

Kids clapped along and shouted even louder than before. And when the band finished, everyone gave them a standing ovation. Mrs. Twinkler couldn't get the kids to stop clapping.

"Don't worry about it," I told Chipmunk. "No problem." I was still sitting on him. "They'll forget Wes Updood when you start to play."

Finally, Feenman and Crench came running down the aisle with Chipmunk's guitar. I climbed up and tugged Chipmunk to his feet. I pulled the guitar over his shoulders.

I gave him a shove toward the stage. "Get up

there, dude!" I said. "You rock! You totally rock!"

Chipmunk staggered onto the stage. His legs were shaking so hard, he looked like he was dancing.

I dropped down into my seat between Feenman and Crench. "We've got a winner," I said. "Check him out. That's what a *winner* looks like!"

Chapter 17

URRRRRP

"Chipmunk, glow and shine!" Mrs. Twinkler said. "A winner has a winning smile!"

Chipmunk couldn't smile. His teeth were chattering too hard.

He raised his guitar. He stared out at the audience.

"Go, dude!" I shouted. "Shake, rattle, and roll!"

But Chipmunk turned and gazed around. "Where's my closet?" he said.

Mrs. Twinkler squinted at him. "Closet?"

"There's no closet," I shouted from the front row. "Just play! Do it, dude! Rock and roll forever!"

Chipmunk's mouth dropped open. "No closet?"

"Go ahead. Never keep an audience waiting," Mrs. Twinkler said.

"But—but—" Chipmunk stared down at me. "I can't play unless I'm in a closet!"

"Chipmunk—do it, dude!" I shouted. "Rock the room!"

He glanced around again. "No closet?" He made a loud *urrp*ing sound. "Bernie, help me. I'm going to hurl. Here comes my lunch. I'm going to *hurl*!"

I jumped from my seat. But I couldn't get onstage in time.

Chipmunk bent over his guitar and hurled his guts out.

When he was finished, I helped him off the stage. I turned to Mrs. Twinkler and flashed her a big smile. "Just a little stage fright," I said. "He'll be great. You'll see."

Urrrrrrrrrrp.

I guessed wrong. Chipmunk wasn't finished. *I'm doomed!* I realized. *DOOMED!*

Chapter 18

URP URP
URPURPURP

The next day I ran into April-May June outside the library. She flashed me a teasing grin, and her blue eyes sparkled. "Too bad you can't come with Wes and me to The Plopps concert," she said. "But I'll tell the Plopp sisters you said hi when I meet them *in person* backstage."

Why did she enjoy torturing me? Didn't she realize she was my girlfriend?

"Don't get your hopes up, April-May," I said. "Bernie B. hasn't given up. I'm still gonna win."

"Ha," she said. "Double ha. How are you going to

win? Chipmunk's big talent is barfing on stage."

"There's a *lot* of other talent in Rotten House," I told her. "I just have to find it."

I hurried to the dorm. I called everyone to a meeting in the Commons Room. I was desperate. I had to find a winning act. The Talent Contest was tomorrow!

I turned to Feenman. "Maybe you, Crench, and Belzer can do your *Three Stooges* act. It was funny. It really had me laughing."

"I don't think so!" Feenman backed away. "You want to see my bruises? I'm bandaged in twelve places!"

"I can't *see* straight!" Crench said. "He poked my eyes out!"

"I'm still *bleeding*!" Belzer wailed. "Please—don't make us!"

"Come on, dudes," I said. "What's a little *pain* when the honor of your dorm is at stake?"

But I could see they wouldn't do it. I glanced around the crowd of guys. "Who else has talent? Anybody else?"

A kid from the first floor, named Mason Dixon,

pushed his way through the crowd. "I've got talent, Bernie. I can gargle all of Hilary Duff's hit songs."

"Awesome!" I said. "Back up. Give him some room. Let's see what he's got."

Mason filled his mouth with water. He started to gargle. It sounded pretty good—until he choked. He choked for about two minutes and swallowed all the water.

"Next!" I cried. "Who else? Who else?"

To my surprise,

Beast pushed a bunch of guys out of his way and stepped up to me. I took a deep breath. Something stank.

"Beast, have you been chasing skunks again?"

He grinned. "Almost caught one. Almost."

I held my nose. "What's your talent?"

"I can burp the love song from *Star Wars*," he said. "Listen. *Urp urp urpurpurp. Urp urpurp urp*—"

"I don't think so," I said. "Anyone else? Anyone?"

Silence.

"Doomed," I muttered. "Doomed." Shaking my head, I slunk back upstairs to my room.

I was halfway up the stairs when I had an *awesome* idea.

Chapter 19

THE BIG SHOW

The next afternoon, I stepped backstage as the Talent Contest started. Was I nervous? Not at all. I was calm as a carrot.

I peeked out from the side of the curtain. Every seat in the auditorium was filled. Every kid in school had turned out to watch my victory.

Mrs. Twinkler called Flora and Fauna Peevish to perform first. "Glow and shine, girls! Glow and shine!"

But they didn't glow and shine. Flora started singing while Fauna was still clearing her throat. So they had to start again. Then Fauna messed up the words.

The two sisters started slapping and hitting each other, and Mrs. Twinkler had to drag them off the stage again.

The kids in the audience were *not* polite. They booed and hissed, and someone tossed a shoe onstage.

Someone tapped me on the shoulder.

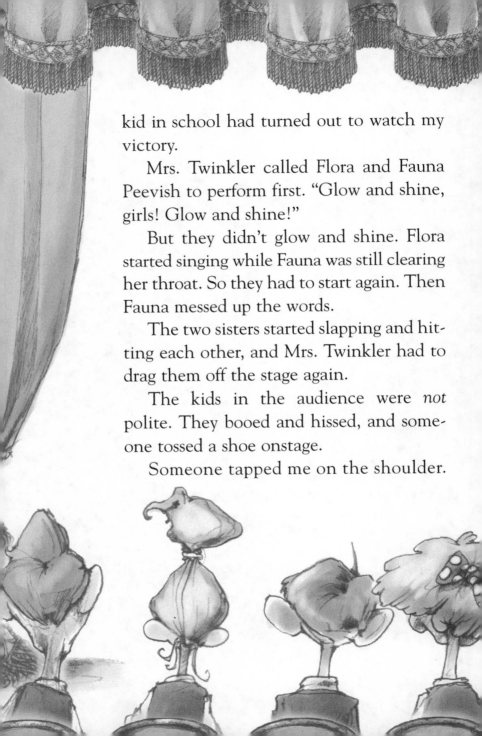

I turned to see Feenman and Crench with big grins on their faces. "Hey, dudes," I said, "how's it going?"

Then I saw that Feenman had a power drill in his hand. "What's up with that?" I asked.

He raised a finger to his lips. "Ssshhh. Bernie," he whispered, "we just drilled a few *extra holes* in Wes Updood's saxophone. He won't notice till he starts to play."

They both giggled.

"Good work," I said. "Wes and his band are up next."

"Where's Chipmunk?" Crench asked.

I pointed behind us. "I've got two guys sitting on him backstage so he won't run away. When I give you the signal, push him

onstage with his guitar."

"But, Bernie, he's just gonna freeze again," Feenman said.

"He'll hurl all over the stage," Crench whispered.

"Don't worry about it," I told him. "I've got it taken care of. Chipmunk is gonna win big-time. And I'm on my way to see The Plopps."

They stared at me with their mouths hanging open. They didn't believe me.

Wes, Sherman, and the Nyce House Band were setting up onstage.

"These cats are really cool!" Mrs. Twinkler was announcing. "They really *swing*. They're going to rock your world!"

Feenman giggled. "Wait till Wes discovers the extra holes in his sax! That'll rock *his* world!"

Crench giggled, too. "He'll blow so hard, his head will explode!"

Sherman pushed a button and started his drumbeats.

Wes stepped to the edge of the stage. "Fried rice, everyone!" he shouted. "Angel hair pasta! Downtown. Downtown!"

So cool.

He took a few steps back and started to play. The band started slowly, picked up steam, then totally rocked.

Watching from the side of the stage, I had to admit it: Wes was *awesome*!

And the extra holes in his sax gave him

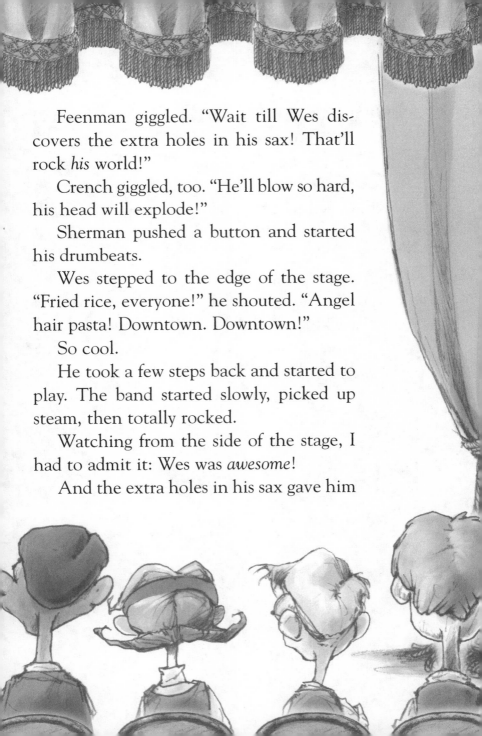

NEW HIGH NOTES! He wailed and trilled the new notes till everyone was *screaming*! They jumped up and danced and rocked to the music. And when it ended, they screamed and stamped their feet for more.

Mrs. Twinkler couldn't get them to stop.

I turned and saw Feenman and Crench shaking their heads sadly. "Sorry, Bernie," Crench said. "We tried. We really did. Better luck next year."

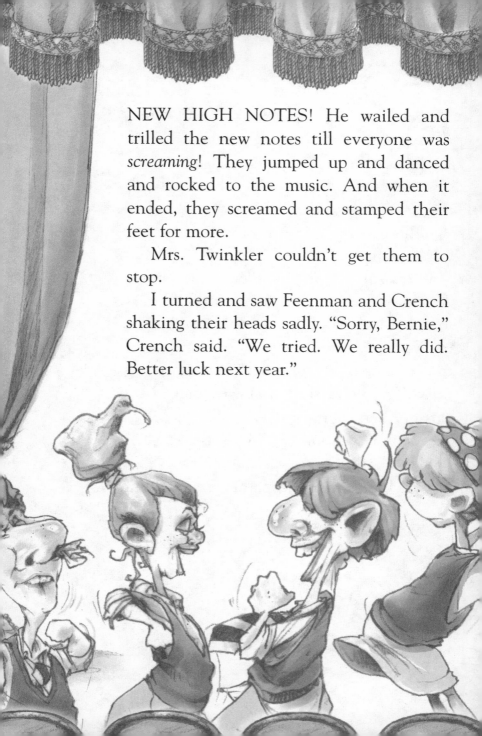

"Are you kidding?" I said. "We're gonna win. Trust me. It's all over. We win!" I pointed to the back. "Hurry. Go get Chipmunk. Strap on his guitar and shove him out there."

Was I nervous now?

You're joking, right?

Calm as a carrot.

I was already daydreaming about what I'd say to the Plopp sisters when I met them....

Chapter 20

WE HAVE A WINNER AND A LOSER!

Chipmunk looked a little dazed. His eyes bulged, and his lips were trembling.

We strapped his guitar on, and all three of us pushed him onstage. His legs were shaking so hard, we actually had to carry him.

"Chipmunk is going to favor us with some guitar stylings!" Mrs. Twinkler told the audience. She smiled at Chipmunk. "Glow and shine now. And don't barf!"

Chipmunk gazed out at the huge crowd of kids. I don't think he heard Mrs. Twinkler. His whole body began to shake and shudder.

The kids thought it was part of the act. They started to clap along.

He turned all around. "Wh-where's my c-closet?" he stammered. "Bernie? My closet?" His eyes suddenly shut. "Uh-oh. I'm going to *hurl*. Where's my closet?"

"HERE'S YOUR CLOSET!" I shouted. I pushed it out onstage.

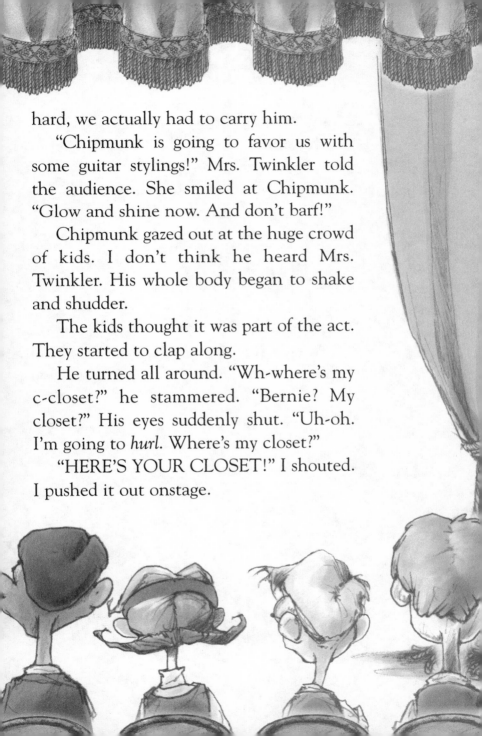

Chipmunk blinked. "My closet?"

"Here it is," I said. "I tore it out of your wall."

Hey—Bernie B. will do *anything* for his guys!

I never saw Chipmunk look so happy. He leaped into the closet, and I slammed the door shut.

I turned to the audience. "Here he is, everyone! The Hidden Guitarist!"

After a few seconds Chipmunk began to twang and rock. Do I have to tell you

what happened next?

His guitar playing was so totally *beyond* awesome, the audience wouldn't let him stop. Every time he ended a song, the audience screamed for more.

The kids were standing on their seats, dancing everywhere, doing cartwheels down the aisle.

Too bad Chipmunk couldn't see it!

He rocked for an hour. And after he stopped, the kids screamed for at least *another* hour!

It took the judges less than ten seconds to decide. CHIPMUNK was the WINNER!

"You did it, Big B! You did it!" Feenman

and Crench shouted, jumping up and down, pumping their fists in the air.

"For sure!" I said. We slapped high fives and low fives, touched knuckles, and did the secret Rotten School Handshake.

I looked around the stage. "Hey—where's Chipmunk?"

Feenman slapped his forehead. "We left him in the closet!"

We ran across the stage,
tugged open the closet door,
and pulled Chipmunk out. "Air!
Air!" he gasped. His face was blue,
but after a few seconds it returned to
the right color.

"Chipmunk, buddy! You won! You won!" I told him, slapping him on the back.

His eyes grew wide. "I did? I won? Oh, wow." He blushed. "I couldn't have done it without you."

April-May came running up to us, her blond hair flying. "Chipmunk—congratulations!" she cried "You're going to The Plopps concert! Congratulations!"

Chipmunk blushed. He grinned at April-May.

"Would you like to go with me?" he asked.

"Yes!" she cried. "I'm there! I'm there! Yes!"

Chipmunk turned to me. "See, Bernie? You're helping me get over my shyness!"

I couldn't breathe. I couldn't talk. Chipmunk and April-May walked off, talking excitedly about the concert.

April-May?

He's taking April-May?

"Hey, Bernie," Feenman called after me. "Hey, wait—Bernie. Where are you going?"

"Where do you think?" I said.

I climbed into the closet and slammed the door.

HERE'S A SNEAK PEEK AT BOOK #6 IN

R.L. STINE'S

ROTTEN SCHOOL

The Heinie Prize

WHY THE TWINS SCREAMED

I hurried to the girls' dorm to find Flora Peevish and her twin sister, Fauna. They hang out a lot with Sherman Oaks, but I didn't care about that tonight. I was desperate.

I found them in their dorm's Commons Room watching Japanese sumo wrestling on TV with a bunch of other girls. The girls were all jumping up and down on the couches, cheering and shouting.

One of them gave me a nice greeting: "Beat it!"

I pointed to the huge dudes in diapers wrestling on TV. "How can you watch those guys?" I asked.

"We think they're cute," she answered.

"Awesome," I said. "You know Belzer, right? You think he's cute, too?"

She stuck her finger down her throat and gagged herself.

"Is that a yes or a no?" I asked.

"Ucccck," her sister said.

I turned to Fauna. "Be honest. What do you think of Belzer?" I asked.

She groaned. "He's like a piece of something you pull out from between your toes."

"So, you have a crush on him?" I said.

"Uccccck."

On TV, the diaper dudes were falling on each other. The girls cheered and shrieked.

I pulled the Peevish twins into the hall. "Look. I need your help," I said. "I'm doing a science experiment. For extra credit in Mr. Boring's class."

"What's the experiment?" Fauna asked.

"I need you to pretend to have *major* crushes on Belzer," I said.

"I'd rather eat cow plop," Flora said.

"Sign me up for that," Fauna said.

I laughed. "Ha-ha-ha. Belzer *loves* girls with a sense of humor!"

"I'm not joking," Flora said. "Bring me the cow plop. I'll show you."

"It's just *pretend*," I said. "Just *pretend* you both have a crush on him. It's an experiment. To build up his confidence. To see if it'll make him change."

"No way," Fauna said, turning up her already-turned-up nose. "Not even pretend."

"I sat next to Belzer at the movies," Flora said, "and he picked his nose the entire time."

"I could hear his stomach growling," Fauna said. "It sounded like he had a cat trapped in there. He burped up some of his lunch and then he *ate* it."

"How about if I bribe you?" I asked.

They stared at me. "What's the bribe?"

"Two six-packs of Foamy Root Beer," I said.

Their eyes lit up. "Two six-packs?" Fauna asked.

I knew they don't drink it. They use it for shampoo because it's so foamy.

"Okay. What do we have to do?" Flora asked.

"Follow me," I said. "Belzer is in the laundry room. Just go in there and make a big fuss over the guy."

"How long do we have to flirt with him?" Fauna asked.

"Give him fifteen minutes. Can you do it?" I asked.

"Ten minutes," Fauna said.

We settled on twelve.

We followed the path across the Great Lawn to the Student Center.

I knew this would help Belzer a lot. Help build his confidence. And I'd make sure to get word to Mrs. Heinie about how popular Belzer was with the girls—because he was so *outstanding*.

The twins followed me through the back door and down the steps to the laundry room. We walked into the bright lights.

And then all three of us gasped. Flora and Fauna opened their mouths—and let out deafening SCREAMS.

Belzer stood there TOTALLY NAKED.

"Belzer? What are you DOING?" I cried.

He shrugged. "Bernie, you told me to wash ALL my clothes!"

ABOUT THE AUTHOR

R.L. Stine graduated from the Rotten School with a solid D+ average, which put him at the top of his class. He says that his favorite activities at school were Scratching Body Parts and Making Armpit Noises.

In sixth grade, R.L. won the school Athletic Award for his performance in the Wedgie Championships. Unfortunately, after the tournament, his underpants had to be surgically removed.

After graduation, R.L. became well known for writing scary book series such as The Nightmare Room, Fear Street, Goosebumps, and Mostly Ghostly, and a short story collection called *Beware!*

Today, R.L. lives in New York City, where he is busy writing stories about his school days.

For more information about R.L. Stine,
go to www.rottenschool.com
and www.rlstine.com